The View from Darien

The View from Darien

Essays on the Teaching of English Literature:

Motive and Method

Don Gutteridge

Afterword by Brian T. W. Way

First Edition

QuodSermo Publishing
www.WetInkBooks.com
QuodSermo@gmail.com

Title: The View from Darien:
Essays on the Teaching of English Literature:
Motive and Method
Author: Don Gutteridge
Afterword: by Brian T. W. Way

Cover Design: Richard M. Grove
Cover Image: With permission from ShutterStock.
Holywell Bay, Cornwall, England UK – by Paul Nash
Layout and Design: Richard M. Grove

Typeset in Garamond
Printed and bound in Canada
Distributed in USA by Ingram,
          – to set up an account – 1-800-937-0152

Library and Archives Canada Cataloguing in Publication

Title: The view from Darien : essays on the teaching of English literature : motive and method /
   Don Gutteridge ; afterword by Brian T.W. Way.
Names: Gutteridge, Don, 1937- author. |
Way, Brian T. W. (Brian Thomas Wesley), 1951- writer of afterword.
Description: 1st edition.
Identifiers: Canadiana 20230158765 |
ISBN 9781989786796 (softcover)
Subjects: LCSH: English literature—Study and teaching.
Classification: LCC PR35 .G88 2023 | DDC 820.71—dc23

Acknowledgements

The author would like to thank the editors of the following periodicals where the articles herein made their first appearance:

- *The English Quarterly* Journal of the Canadian Council of Teachers of English

- *Indirections* Journal of the Ontario Council of Teachers of English

- *Journal of Canadian Studies*

- *Classmate* Journal of the Manitoba Teachers of English Association

- *English Journal* Journal of the National Council of Teachers of English (US)

Dedicated to

Colm O Sullivan:

teacher, scholar, friend:

In Memoriam

Table of Contents

. . . like stout Cortez when with eagle eyes

He star'd at the Pacific—and all his men

Look'd at each other with a wild surmise—

Silent, upon a peak in Darien.

– 01 –

Truth and Consequences:
Selecting Literature

Part 1 – The Rudderless Ark

In the spring of 1988 the Ontario Ministry of Education decided to develop a position paper on the subject of selecting and using controversial literature in English classrooms from Kindergarten to OAC. An advisory committee was struck to launch the project, and each member was asked to prepare a position paper in advance of the first meeting. I wrote one focusing on grades 7 to 10—but with clear implications for the upper grades as well. Eighteen months later a working group under the Ministry's direction produced a discussion paper (M.O.E., 1989) entitled *The Selection and Use of Literature in Elementary and Secondary Schools*. It was a pale reflection of the lively and contentious debate which marked that first meeting of the advisory group in 1988, a group composed of teachers, professors, administrators and poets.

The Discussion Paper (not, it is useful to note, an official guideline or support document, and hence lacking any real legal punch) does, in general, recapitulate the time-honoured goals for literature as providing vicarious experience, opening up the possibilities of empathy with 'other experience' and values, meeting the imperatives of cultural (and multi-cultural) literacy, in addition to its obvious functional role in developing literacy skills *per se* (see pp. 5-7). Even the teacher's role is defined somewhat in terms of having to nudge students to see alternatives and develop critical awareness-with the teacher mediating the results; she is even allowed as being central to the selection process itself (pp. 8-11).

Fair enough. However, all of this good work is instantly undone by the authors' immediate reversion to tired and tiresome exhortations to *local boards* to find their own balance (by juggling? high-speed alternation?) among the competing elements of these goals and to the platitudinous but problematic constraints of gender equity, multicultural diversity, our multipath society, *etc.* (p. 8). This is followed by a checklist, that ought to daunt the most determined English teacher, detailing the dangers of offending remarks in literature selections related to religion, race, ethnic group, the handicapped, sexual orientation or graphic violence (pp. 12-13). This minefield is then disingenuously disarmed by blithe reference to unhelpful but trendy teaching jargon about theories of personal and variable interpretation, about the historical relativity of all literature (no universality here!), and about meaning-as-constructed-by-the-kids anyway (so why worry?), and so on (pp. 13-15). Beyond mediation, the teacher is somehow "to foster and prompt" students' early responses towards "deeper meanings" (p. 15). Further, the teacher is urged to "seize the 'teachable moment' ... and assist students" to examine "alternative or even, competing viewpoints within the framework of today's expected value systems" (p. 16, emphasis added).

This is as close as the document comes to admitting the inherent tensions and contradictions within its own stated goals, but, of course, the italicized addendum undercuts them anyway. What are "today's expected value systems"? If they are multiple, how can literature be used inoffensively? Whose expectations are referred to-those of the Ministry, the local board, the parents, the teacher? Do we eliminate author-viewpoints not within our accepted values? Student viewpoints that are not "acceptable?" Worse still, no illustrations or operational suggestions for implementation are provided for the specific guidance of the pitiable local boards who must navigate these treacherous seas in their rudderless ark.

What follows is an edited version of my 1988 position paper, recast now as advice to the Ministry on which crucial aspects of the topic—choosing and using controversial literature—it should include in any future documents for English teachers, whether these be guidelines, pro-files or resource pamphlets. Part one deals with the prior issue of goals and values, one which both muddied and enlivened our original debate; Part 2 will focus directly on the kinds of controversy necessarily entailed by attention to proper goals and values, and will conclude with a set of specific principles for selecting powerful literary texts in grades 7 to 12/OAC.

The Ministry's Role

The Ontario Ministry of Education sets the overarching goals for literature study and tacitly approves the values embedded in both the goals and the literature. In an open society like ours, it does not have a 'free hand'; quite rightly it tries to balance the wishes of society (diffuse as they may be) against the ontological imperatives of the 'thing being encountered in schools' (poem, exoskeleton, accounts of the Battle of Lundy's Lane, Archimedes' principle). To give a recent example of how these extreme positions can occur in their raw state, I note the Darwinian/Creationist controversy. The Ministry may decree the Creationist view of our origins to be part of science courses, but that does not make them scientific-given the current ontological status of science in our world. (Neo-Marxists, of course, have other views of the matter, but he majority of the Ontario public, for now, is apt to side with the biologists at U. of T.).[1] In such cases, the Ministry must either look foolish or be condemned by certain religious lobby groups. In literature studies, the Ministry may decree a sonnet to be a haiku, but that doesn't change the accepted norms. The point here, at the onset, is that the Ministry's role in setting goals for a subject inevitably involves shuttling between the demands for coherent social policy and the realities, givens and consequences of those policies in actual classrooms. The Ministry's role, then, is always more valuative (normative) than it is instrumental.

The values of literature, in society at large and hence by extrapolation in our classrooms, are both cultural and empirical. As Ontarians, we read novels, go to plays, see films, read and write reviews, contribute to literary criticism, use literature for both personal and cultural (sociological and political) purposes. Hence, a body of practice has built up which in turn establishes ongoing cultural norms. These have both an idiosyncratic aspect (our own peculiar ways of 'using' literature) and a more general one (common features shared by citizens in the U.S., the U.K., and elsewhere). While some of us believe also that there are innate aspects of response to, and the use of, literary/symbolic materials, this notion is highly contested. So, unlike the biologists, we ought not to base our stand on ontological or 'scientifically' demonstrable defenses (neat as they may be). Nonetheless, cultural behaviour (including embedded values and unarticulated ideals/goals/hopes) is 'real' and is historically evolved. The Ministry, using its experts and its political sensitivities, must then establish curriculum goals for literature teaching which take into account the general ways in which literature has been received and used in Western Societies and the specific ways in Ontario.[2]

None of this is new or revolutionary, but it bears repetition because at the moment Ontario society is changing, is more diverse, and has more effective political pressure groups than ever before. (Note the 'banning' of *The Merchant of Venice* in Waterloo County, despite a superb defense of it by the English teachers within the Ministry's own guidelines and long-accepted practice.) There is real temptation to make 'quick fixes' in the way literature is to be used. Two general pressures are worth noting. The multicultural and feminist aspects of Ontario society (real enough, legitimate enough) would suggest a simple 'adjustment' of kinds of books to be used in English and some of the kinds of questions arranged around them. As we will see this is not a simple process at all, though properly conceived some of the intentions can be, and are being, met. The other major pressure is towards the instrumental side of English, bolstered by the public clamour for better English, good citizenship, life skills, and job-related (good) 'behaviours'. The Ministry has to some extent given way to both pressures-as reference to the goals in The Discussion Paper show-and hence has itself created ambiguity and some doubt in the profession about the nature of the goals and values for literature teaching.

In brief, the Ministry perceives itself to be 'selecting from the culture' (as it should) when it responds to direct pressures to broaden and alter the way literature is to operate in English classrooms. But the cultural norms for the use of literature and the way in which we hope our children will respond to it have historical roots. In their essence, they change very slowly, being embedded in long-held 'Western· ways of responding-to-texts and in the in-built time-lag between contemporary social trends and the production of authentic texts by mature writers, here and elsewhere. Moreover, both writers and readers have historically operated in the context of a literature that includes Chaucer, Shakespeare, Hemingway and Margaret Laurence. These arc powerful cultural 'givens' which, if they are to 'give way' to pressing social changes and needs, will not do so easily and not without immense dislocation of every kind—psychological, pedagogical, ethical and curricular. There are five thousand or more literature teachers in Ontario whose education and professional lives have been based on broadly held, culturally supported norms over many decades. Moreover, almost all new teachers headed into English teaching in grades 7-12/OAC and many of those going into K-6 Language Arts have been similarly acculturated in both school and university. In addition, these teachers have grown up in an Ontario society where Canadian literature and culture has been so dominant as to seem almost 'natural'. Put plainly, if the contemporary English teacher is to be sea-changed into a collaborator or coach, a nudger or assister. such remodelling will be made against culturally acquired behaviours that have already been deeply internalized. It is, then, these cultural realities which a beleaguered Ministry must balance off against the urgent demands of pressure groups for instant reform and quick fixes.

Value-Shifts in English

None of the above is meant to suggest that literature teaching in Ontario has not changed significantly since 1962 (the Robarts year).

It has. For example, one could read B.C. Diltz's *Patterns of Surmise* (1962), the pedagogical text of the 1950s and early 60s, and my own Brave Season (1983) to get some idea of the shifts in methodology and, to a lesser extent, in the value-aspects of 'learning' literature. Unfortunately, we lack any detailed account of our own historical curriculum development, which has left us vulnerable to both societal pressures and foreign fads. Figure I is a summary I recently made of both the changed and retained features of literature teaching in Ontario from the era of Diltz (1950s) to the 1980s, the Post-Diltzian period which lasted more or less until the 1987 1-S English guideline.

The changes have been substantial, reflecting both the shift in Ministry policies and the province's cultural norms in regard to the uses, pleasures and values of reading. It should be pointed out, also, that between the 1964 guideline: *English and Senior English: 1977*—when most of the changes took place—there was no new Ministry guideline to sanction them (there was tacit support, some resource documents, and a largely ignored,

---

Value Shift: 1960-1980

Common Retaine Features
Diltz/Post-Diltz

– text as art-speech
– text/genre integrity
– moral-aesthetic student response
– lived-through encounters
– teacher as model-reader, mediator, expert
– intrinsic text-specific questions
– opponent of stock-question/stock-response, wholly
private interpretation, social science themes

Modern Features

Diltz	*Post-Diltz*
– all mediation/questioning during classroom encounters	– mediation/questioning extended beyond the classroom, before and after the encounter
– little comparative/unit work (thematic or generic)	– genre and theme units with generic or text integrity
– no explicit developmental features or stages of growth	– range of questions/tasks/modes of expression vis a vis texts of various depth, with potential for development or stage features
– consistent with student experience	– applied to and modified by students' personal and social experience
– stock, generic and mismatched test and exam questions	– evaluation linked to unit goals with potential for integration, and for matching task and format
– little planned transfer (always highly controlled)	– variety of planned transfer: group individual study, essays, seminars, presentations

---

intellectually impoverished guideline in 1969 for *Intermediate English*). One must conclude that the movement away from entrenched Diltzian methods-reinforced until 1967 by provincial examinations set by university professors-was in large part a 'natural' evolution initiated by, and representative of the views of, literature teachers themselves. (Numerous faddish forays and educationally trendy gambits also occurred; like transformational grammar, film-replacing-book, McLuhan and mass media, and gritty social-science theme units.) Hence, we have ample precedent for curriculum change which evolves—slowly—

with the consent of the teachers and the public, and during which the specious and ephemeral are winnowed out.

In regard to the latter phenomenon, we must also infer that this sorting process was aided not so much by Ministry policy as by a strong sense on the part of teachers of what inherited values and procedures were abiding—culturally, educationally and pragmatically. The upper section of Figure I clearly indicates this abiding set of goals, values and beliefs and, of course, the pedagogics likely to be consonant with them. I would hazard a guess that-despite numerous differences in approaches, in styles, in the mixture of old-and-new (the left-right columns in the chart)-the vast majority of current English teachers – provincially, nationally and intemationally[3] -would agree upon the seven common features mentioned.

But by 1988 the question had become whether or not this irreducible core of accepted cultural norms was still Ministry policy or not. If it was to be altered to fit more pressing social imperatives, then teachers needed to know precisely where, why and how. [The 'return' to the more ancient set suggested by the 1989 Discussion Paper, only two years after their near-deletion from I/S English: 1987, is more puzzling than helpful.)

A Necessary Balance

To the majority of English teachers, then, a core of beliefs and values has always been extant and widely accepted. Other aspects of our work are more idiosyncratic, and not all teachers interpret the core values in exactly the same way. Indeed, these values in and of themselves create an inevitable set of tensions and call for the art of delicate balancing. The best summary of how this necessary balance-in-tension has got distorted elsewhere is to be found in David Allen's English Teaching Since 1965: How Much Growth?[4] (see Figure 2). The tension between adult and child, public and private, cultural and personal, received knowledge and evolving knowledge is vividly and compellingly presented in Allen's work. Moreover, he makes it clear that the 'balanced' elements are really parts of the same phenomenon: they cannot be juggled or alternated easily; their very tension is one of the sources of literature's power over us. Finally, Allen accurately describes the conditions, constraints and other realities that English teachers live with day-to-day-the phenomenological quality singularly missing from Ministry policy documents over the years. Whatever else the Ministry decides to put in any future policy statements about the selection and use of literature, it must include a statement in the spirit of Figure 2, in which the role of literature in general is defined in ordinary, professionally compre-hensible language. In the least, the Ministry should be aware that Allen's overview does register the only genuine consensus among contemporary teachers.

1987: The Double Agenda

Such a movement was signaled, of course, in 1-S English: 1987. The double-centred, two-columned 'introduction' on page 2 is alas representative of an ambiguity that permeates what is still the governing document for all Ontario English teachers in grades 7-12. While the "Centrality of Literature" column is consonant with both Senior English: 1977 and the kind of consensus outlined in Figure 2, it sits as an isolated set of gestures amid a more formidable second agenda: the predominant (and prior) column on language development as "the central focus"; and repeated calls for life-skills, for the deconstruction of mass media, for personal growth, for good citizen-ship, for collaborative learning. and, it follows, for a much-reduced authority for teachers. While many of these worthwhile initiatives can be made compatible with a literature-driven (not centered) programme and with the demanding and risky moral, ethical and psychological goals implicit in the literature column (and attested to by two generations of excellent teachers), they are not so integrated in the guideline itself. Nor is there any admission of potential loss and gain. We need not argue the niceties of interpretation here because the confusion in the field over this essential point-where does literature stand'?-is empirically demonstrable and is continuing. The fact that of the seventeen Pro-File support documents only two seem to have much to say about literature has not gone un-remarked. Whatever *I-S English*: 1987 meant to convey, it has not provided an answer to this first-order question.

Moreover, setting the new goals for English among the thirteen "Provincial Goals of Education" (pp. 5-7) merely added to the confusion, not in the least by diffusing the English goals even further and thus encouraging any pressure-group at all to apply the screws to what must appear to it to be a discrete and isolatable aspect of the programme. For example, fitness buffs could argue for more drama, it appears: Goal #4 states: "Through dramatization ... students respond physically and imaginatively to course content." Environmentalists would be heartened by Goal #12 to press for 'literature' units on ecology or acid rain. The work-a-day pragmatists will be inspired by Goal #II to insist that punctuality, meeting deadlines and keeping work-diaries be made mandatory aspects of all courses. Family Life enthusiasts will be pleased to make suggestions regarding Goal #7 ("Develop an understanding of the role of the individual within the family"), with specific advice no doubt about suitable text selections. The point here is not that any of these overarching aims lack value (or even clarity) nor that they do-here and there—often become part of our work in English; but rather that these discrete statements convey a falsely fragmented and diffuse picture of the central, ongoing and essential goals of an English programme. They suggest that key elements do not play off against one another as parts of a whole, and that they are often definable only in the whole context of our teaching procedures, in terms of the age and abilities of students, and against the precipitate demands of the texts themselves. Somehow, in any new document, the Ministry must publicly convey that English is not a set of infinitely separable objectives, activities and methods in which parts can be interchanged with impunity, can be attached independently to specific socially-cozy objectives, or can be textually aligned and streamlined to fit narrow interests, however legitimate. Reading literature is a single set of interrelated acts, whichever 'school' of critical response one happens to espouse. Paradoxically, the Ministry itself appears to have accepted the Whole-Language principle (always held, however restrictedly, by all good English teachers—even Diltz), which certainly embodies the notion of integrated elements. In fact, the official call for integration is now more than fifteen years old.[5]

Whatever the intention of the preamble to 1-S English: 1977, the contradictory double-centre statements, the linguistic-sociological bias of its contents, and the fuzzy clichés about the fit between English studies and the Provincial Goals of Education have led only to confusion. Moreover, in regard to the selection of controversial literature, I-S English: 1987 has set the door agape for every lobby-group in Ontario. It is precisely in this muddled context that the Ministry's Discussion Paper *The Selection and Use of Literature in Elementary and Secondary Schools* must be read. Nothing short of a new official guideline will do to provide the clarity required to even begin addressing how controversial literature is to be selected and used by working teachers in actual schools. With this m mmd, I offer the following preliminary advice.

Recommendations Re: Statement of Goals and Values

The Ministry of Education in any future policy document should:

1 – Use the kind of consensus indicated in the work of Allen and in its own guidelines-Senior English.: 1977, 1979; 1-S *English:* 1987, p. 8 and p. 2: ("The Centrality of Literature "); and Selection and Use, pp. 4-7-to write, in continuous prose, a statement of the general purposes of literature in grades 7- 12/0AC. These shall be fundamental first-order goals only. 2 – Include in this statement an acknowledgement of the normal and healthy tensions involved in handling high-powered literature: between the demands of text and the personal response of students, between public standards of 'interpretation' and idiosyncratic readings, between the necessity for sustained attentiveness and the student's right to choose or reject, and so on. 3. Unambiguously acknowledge the teacher's role as expert and as public adjudicator-constrained. by the need to respect privacy, individual response, and initiative; to mediate psychologically hazardous situations; and to show due respect to the text itself[6] 4. Include a statement, comprehensible to the general public, about the meaning of the holistic principle. For example, that reading a class novel in grade 7 or grade 12 means that certain ordinary, contextual, unfragmented sets of activities be guaranteed the student as first-order priorities; that is, reasonable time to read, reflect, talk, confer, write about the text as a whole; teacher-prompted tasks with some student choice and appropriate evaluation by the teacher; and freedom to respond to and extend ideas from the text, constrained only by the need for focused attention and

the particular language of the text. With such uncontaminated guarantees, teacher and students will be freed to do any of the 'other' socially worthwhile things suggested (however remotely) by the study of a literary work. A statement of this kind is crucial: without it, any policy document will be intrinsically flawed. How to select and use controversial literature in Intermediate-Senior English is embedded in the prior question of programme goals. Until it is clear as to what these goals are and what imperatives they place upon text selection and pedagogy, any discussion of controversial issues or censorship is debatable only in a theoretical vacuum. Part 2 of this article will go on to delineate a small set of common goals (in the absence of same from the Ministry) and from them develop arguments and a set of operating principles for selecting and using controversial literature.

Endnotes

1 – I refer here to the influence of recent deconstructionist criticism and semiotics as well as phenomenology and the Neo-Marxist notions of 'socially constructed' knowledge. See, for example, Corcoran and Evans (1987) for a variety of these dissenting opinions regarding the traditional norms and canons of reading literature.

2 – See Kieran Egan, *Educational Development*, pp. 102-110 for an intelligent discussion of the culture-bound nature of education and child development.

3 – For a very similar set of goals in the U.K. at about the same time, see John Dixon, *Education /6-19: The Role of English and Communication* (1979. pp. 46-49). For further discussion see Gutteridge (1982). There is, of course. another whole set of instrumental arguments to he made for keeping literature not only at the centre of the course but as its impelling force. Instead of, or in addition to, the prime facie cultural goals for literature—the focus of this paper-one could argue that if the schools' first job is to have kids 'language' better, and, in particular, learn to talk and write and think in a more personally responsible way. then using powerful literary texts to drive the expressive/experiential features of such a programme is at least a viable option. That is, Writing Process, Interactive Learning and Collaborative Learning are not the only means to a more 'linguistic' focus in the curriculum. The work of Holdaway (1979, 1984) has definitely demonstrated that a literature driven programme, even in K-3. can do it all. *Brave Season* (Gutteridge, 1983) is an attempt to show how the same principles can work at the grades 7-10 level.

4 – Sec in particular Allen (1970), chs. 7-11.

5 – See Ontario Ministry of Education, PIJ1: 1975, *passim*. Curiously enough, yet another support document (i.e., one lacking legal punch) post 1977 seems in places to return to the older set of goals for literature and to the 1971 conception of integrated Language Arts; *see Growing With Books* M.O.E., 1988), particularly the contributions of Aitken, of Booth, Phenix and Swartz, and of Lissa Paul (in the "Prologue" and "Epilogue" to Book I). These, alas, are undercut – inadvertently'? mischievously? – by the contributions of Wells and others. Nonetheless the impression left by the five booklets taken as a whole is clearly one of reaffirmation in the aesthetic values of the "classics". The term 'literature' is used on almost every page-without a blush or wince.

6 – For an example of how a statement of interlocking principles can be composed—including goals, teacher's role, text-selection criteria, and basic teaching regimes see Gutteridge (1983, pp. 10-14) where the same set is configured first for Primary and then for Junior and intermediate grades.

Bibliography

– Allen, D. (1980). *English Teaching Since 1965: How Much Growth?* London. UK: Heinemann.

– Corcoran, B. and Evans, E., Eds. (1987). *Readers, Texts, Teachers.* Upper Montclair. NJ: Boynton/Cook.

– Diltz, B.C. (1962). *Patterns of Surmise.* Toronto, ON: Clarke Irwin.

– Dixon, J. (1979). *Education /6-/9: The Role of English and Communication. London.* UK: Macmillan Education.

– Egan, K. (1979). *Educational Development.* New York: Oxford University Press.

– Gutteridge, D. (1982). "The View from Darien: The Drama of Literature in the High School Classroom," *The English Quarterly*, V, 2, 3-14.

– Gutteridge, D. (1983). *Brave Season: Reading and the Language Arts in Grade Seven to Ten.* London, ON: The Althouse Press.

– Holdaway, D. (1979). *The Foundations of Literacy.* Sydney, AU: Ashton-Scholastre.

– Holdaway, D. (1974). *Stability and Change in Literacy Learning.* London, ON: The Althouse Press.

– Ontario Ministry of Education (1964). RPS4 English. Toronto.

– Ontario Ministry of Education (1969). Intermediate English. Toronto.

– Ontario Ministry of Education (1976). P/1/, The Formative Years. Toronto.

– Ontario Ministry of Education (1977). English, Senior Division. Toronto.

– Ontario Ministry of Education (1987). Intermediate-Senior English. Toronto.

– Ontario Ministry of Education (1988). "Growing With Books: Children's Literature in the Formative Years and Beyond." II vols. Toronto.

– Ontario Ministry of Education (1989). "The Selection and Use of Literature in Elementary and Secondary Schools, A Discussion Paper for the Development of Policies and Procedures in Ontario School Board." Toronto.

Part 2 – The Pleasures of Controversy

First-Oruer Goals

In Part I I argued that the Ministry's most recent goal statements for literature teaching in grades 7-12/0AC are at best diffuse and scattered, and at worst ambiguous and vulnerable to narrow public lobbying. The development of any set of principles for selecting controversial literary texts and dealing with the consequences must be predicated upon the Ministry's *clear re-statement of its long-promulgated goals in this area,* including reference to *the role of the teacher* and a *guarantee of the holistic principle* (in unit-design and in the achievement of first-order goals).

While not necessarily complete, the selection below (from *l-S English: 1987,* p. 8) constitute such a set of first-order goals. They are also the ones most likely to raise public controversy, and (happily)those least vulnerable to piecemeal lobbying:

Through interaction with their peers and the teacher, students shall have opportunities to:

1 – develop a lifelong love of reading;

2 – understand and enjoy literature and appreciate its significance in the history of human experience and imagination;

3 – become aware of themselves as readers and come to realize the worth and uniqueness of their own responses;

4 – understand the role that language, literature, and the media play in the exploration of intellectual issues and in the establishment of personal and societal values;

5 – develop critical skills and use them to respond to ideas communicated through the various media.

My editing of these 1987 goal statements is deliberate. I have omitted the goals related to writing proficiency, to careers, to citizenship. to self-directed learning, and to multiculturalism. These are not without importance but-sprinkled as they are among those above- they suggest that there is not only no priority here (another *list?)* but little or no necessary interdependency. Conversely, this edited group are a *related set* and as such may be sanctioned as first-order objectives. The other goals may be worthwhile and may even he a legitimate part of English, but they flow from, or arc only tangentially related to, the focused study of literary texts.

In the literature-study 'set', then, both goals and consequent demands on selection principles now become dear. as does the potential for controversy. For example, "a lifelong love of reading" (Goal # 1) implies that teachers will have to promote broadly based student reading for personal pleasure. While books of literary and ethical value can and will he encouraged by teachers, the latitude of choice essential to achieving the immediate goal (personal engagement and independent selection) and its long-range extension (a lifelong reading habit). may occasionally result in students reading, in class during USSR [Uninterrupted Silent Sustained Reading] or at home, hooks which could be judged as meretricious, dangerously fantastic, bigoted, or even obscene. Obviously, here, a distinct set of guidelines needs to be developed for *Unsupervised Personal Reading,* one which gives teachers clear parameters and control procedures reasonably consistent with the goal. If it cannot be approached uncontroversially through 'free reading', then Goal #I must be altered by the Ministry. At present, teachers and principals are in a vulnerable position.

"To have students understand, enjoy and appreciate the significance of literature in human experience and imagination" (Goal #2) is one of the abiding sets of goals for English-here and elsewhere. It mandates the role of the teacher as selector of literary texts (literary knowledge and appropriateness are requisite here) and as one who must *compel* sustained exposure to powerful texts. Moreover, the intellectual grasp of, and response to, the imaginative, mind-stretching and morally challenging qualities of culturally representative texts chosen and arranged and task-directed by the teacher-will inevitably raise controversy. First, such texts are chosen for *all* students (or, in the least, small groups with some individual choice) because sustained attention, focused inter-peer talk, shared responses, debate with teacher and 'author'-all are *required* if the goal is to be achieved. Whatever the particular text, if it be a representative 'classic' with the power to engage, to intellectually extend, to hold attention, and to incite debate, some part of it is bound to affect some students disproportionately or inappropriately. For example, the text may be centred on, or appear to be centred on, racial themes (*Huckleberry Finn),* ethnic clashes *(The Merchant of Venice),* religious issues *(The Power and the Glory).* social values *(The Catcher in the Rye),* or narrow ethnic experience *(Under the Ribs of Death).* Christian, Jew, Black, Hungarian, suburbanite, working-class kid-someone will be offended.

Here, it will be a question of defending our choice-of-text directly on literary/aesthetic grounds, for the goal-applicable from grades 7 to 12/*OAC*-implies that the literary text must be powerful enough in its language, structure, representation of experience and ambiguity to provoke the responses needed to address the far-reaching implications of the goal—"significance in the history of human experience". By the same token, it compels the active involvement of the teacher in the text selection, in the setting of tasks, in the adjudication of ongoing responses, and in the mediation of controversies within the class itself. Giving kids free choice of text or open-ended tasks, or calling it all 'independent study'—these ploys will not work to meet the particular demands of this goal, even though they might help diffuse any controversy. While we can never absolutely defend the selection of one specific text over another (*A Jest of God* over, say, *Duddy Kravitz),* we can (and must) reserve the right to select one *kind* of text over another (for instance, *Jaws* will not help students achieve this goal as well as *The Stone Angel* will). In brief, this goal is an inherently controversial one, and defensible selection criteria must be established if it is to be preserved intact. Whatever value obtains for the more recent Ministry thrust towards student independence and collaboration, it neither supersedesnor mitigates the effects of-a prior, first-order goal like #2, above. The retention of this traditional goal in *I-S: English 1987* would seem to indicate the Ministry's faith in *its unique contribution*

"Become aware of themselves as readers and come to realize the worth and uniqueness of their own responses" (Goal #3) leads to a further kind of controversy. This goal is more 'contemporary' in that it calls upon teachers to have students do more talking. more small group discussion, more reflection on their own processes, more self-evaluation, and more *responding-through* personal journals among other things. And while it raises issues similar to those in Goal #2, Goal #3 seems less intrinsically controversial, because more personal choice, more independent study, and more casual interaction with teacher and peers—these student-mediated actions would appear to be sufficient to address the goal adequately. Put another way, this goal does not seem to *compel* shared, focused, *sustained* moral/ ethical/ intellectual response to a psychologically risky and ambiguous literary text selected by the teacher (as a stand-in for the culture'!). However, even if no single group be 'offended by' a literary text or other book encountered under this set of goals (much of the reading will he self-selected and much response unprompted), the goal nonetheless tacitly urges the teacher to *press* students for *some* kind of response, for some level of engagement in group discussion (to 'test' the *worth* of their own responses?), for some commitment *vis a vis* the evolving ethos or value position of the text to which they have decided to respond. How far, then, do we press? Force disclosure? Eavesdrop on journal responses? Assign grades for active participation in the discussion of moral issues'! While these kinds of controversies have been, so far, less prone to public scrutiny, because they are essential to one of our first-order goals, we shall still have need to develop principles for dealing with any sort of mandated discussion and personal response through journals, writing folders and group-work.

Goal #4 above raises controversies similar to Goal #2 (it is really a complementary goal and ought to be conflated with the latter). Goal #5, while related to #2 and #4, deserves to be treated separately in regard to the question of controversy. In order "to develop critical skills", students will need to experience two essential things—both likely to prove controversial. First, one cannot he critical—that is. evaluate phenomena with discrimination—unless one has knowledge of a particular field (including, of course, personal knowledge) and its range of possibilities,[1] *some of which brought by* design *to run counter to a student's current beliefs and attitudes.* In literature teaching we choose-even for grade 7's-novels that arc morally or experientially or ideologically *ambiguous:* they can he interpreted in more than one way. Which raises the second point: one student will invariably disagree with another student, with a character in the story, with the teacher (playing surrogate author?), [2] with himself or herself (on a subsequent occasion), and so on. Without public issues and cumulative knowledge and understanding, our students cannot be properly critical, nor can they learn to cherish their own beliefs. In short, critical thinking is not a set of instrumental skills, nor an habitual 'learned' attitude, nor a value-neutral form of logic. If this is so, then the English teacher will be obliged to have students deliberately *engage* ethically ambiguous material (see Gutteridge. 1983, pp. 69-74). to have them take public stands on issues, and to promote vigorous group interaction on these. Hence, Goal #5 has great potential to provoke controversy. Challenging, ambiguous material—even if it escapes 'offending' in the obvious ways (sex, profanity. violence)—will. during the sustained attention it receives, lead to students taking value positions which some parents might find unpalatable or objectionable. And again the teacher's need to *press* for engagement. for disclosure, for an exchange of views, and at the same time to *protect* the students' privacy, their vulnerable sensibilities, or even the general ethical norms of Ontario society—this necessary dichotomy can easily be mishandled in the classroom or he mis-read by a well-meaning public.

Taking the Ministry at its own word, then, in terms of its own somewhat hazily promulgated objectives and in light of the self-evident and necessary aspects of controversy raised by these objectives, one can begin to formulate some recommendations for the next round of goal formulation or guideline writing.

A – Recommendations for a Ministry Policy on
The Role of Controversial Literature in the
English Classroom

1 – Following the outline of first-order goals suggested above, the Ministry shall explain clearly the necessity for both ambiguous, morally challenging and psychologically hazardous literary texts (from grades 7-12/0AC) and the dual responsibility of literature teachers to press and protect-if the goals are to be met. If this principle can be acknowledged, explained, and defended-then working criteria for the 'rules and constraints' that obtain (relative to age, grade and programme) can be subsequently developed.

2 – If the Ministry feels that adequate rules and constraints cannot he developed in light of the above desiderata, then it ought to modify the goals to exclude authentic literature from the English curriculum. *Under no circumstances should the Ministry equivocate on this issue by:*

– indicating that there is available an alternative group of inherently uncontroversial literary texts (free of offensive sex, profanity, violence, gender bias-which items, while part of literature's 'controversial quality·, are *not* the essential, radical part thereof).

– suggesting (as the "19H7 Guideline-with-Pro-files" docs, here and there) that the teacher's role to press-and-protect has now been softened to that of coach, cheerleader, facilitator (sweet but harmless) and concomitantly that the range of student choice (collaborating not only on what topics but which goals) is now broad enough so as to virtually eliminate 'compelled engagement'.

3 – Irrespective of any decisions taken on the two recommendations above, the Ministry should explain to the public the reasons behind the wide personal reading programme (which will go on regardless of what happens to literature) out of which, again, a distinct set of rules and constraints' can then he developed.

Principle into Practice

Once a set of first-order goals is established and once the necessary risks and contro-versial consequences have been acknowledged and officially ratified, then the question of deductively elaborating a set of operating principles for selection, for appropriate teaching and even for board-level implementation becomes tenable. In 1989 I was asked by the Ministry of Education to propose a set of such principles and procedures. What follows is a version of that proposal, developed initially for grades 7 to 10 (my area of interest) but easily adapted to include grades 1 to 12/0AC as well. The suggestions here assume that the first-order goals and their inherently controversial consequences have been given official sanction.

A. Principles of Text Selection In Grades 7-12

1. Core Texts: Whole-Class or Small-Group Discussion,

Teacher-Mediated

The novel* shall:

1.1 be linguistically and rhetorically rich, worthy of being read aloud, generally at an independent reading level well above the class median, and/or a story that repays repeated 'readings'. (It does not have to be a received 'classic' so long as these values arc present.) It should meet the Ministry's stated criteria as a work of the imagination.

To avoid repetition and to emphasize the general nature of the criteria. I have used the novel to stand for all genres. More detailed genre-specific criteria could he readily developed.

1.2 contain characters, themes, issues and moral questions (suited to the age, reading experience and background of the students). worthy of sustained attention and with enough ambiguity to incite more than one interpretation.

1.3 be capable—given appropriate teaching—of honestly engaging students' attention so that wherever possible they will be able to say they 'enjoyed' it or, in the least, respected it as providing a worthwhile experience. There should be potential for powerful psychological identification with characters and issues; e.g., growing up, family relationships, self and society.

1.4 despite its ambiguity or controversial 'themes', not—in concert with other materials on the course—seriously undermine the guiding ethos of our society. Put another way, the novel *as a whole* shall not have as its *principal* focus, as its *prevailing* ethos, or as its *unambiguous* 'message' matter which is patently contradictory to Ontario norms; e.g., the promotion of racial hatred, the ridicule of religion, the exploitation of minorities. This does *not* mean that the novel will be free of characters or individual statements or even offensive language conveying objectionable views: without these there could be no conflict, no ambiguity, and no need for reflection, guided talk and further reading. The operative terms here are: as a whole, principal, prevailing, unambiguous.

[At the senior level or with selected gifted classes in grades 9 and 10, this principle may be relaxed for individual works but ought to apply across units and courses: wall-to-wall Black Comedy would violate the principle here. As well, in grades II and 12 model considerations need also to be considered: e.g., in romance characters are unambiguous. In grade 7 to 10, where romance is the chief form of independent personal reading, it is imperative that class novel—though they have the shape of romance—be ambiguous and thematically dense.

1.5 not be chosen *principally* to serve second-order goals or considcrations; such as, multiculturalism, sex-role stereotyping, life-skills. sex education, targeted social problems (divorce, single parenthood). While these aspects will often be a part of the study of the novel, they are not to be its central concern. In particular, such *a priori* 'social' objectives often lead to the selection of cooked hooks·, unambiguous pot-boilers or even exploitative fiction.

2. Independent Personal Reading:

Student – Selected

School – Sanctioned

The novel shall:

2.1 be freely chosen by the student from the classroom 'library', the resource centre, the public library, or home (or may he purchased).

2.2 not violate the norms of the student's family (if they object, other choices will he offered, since unlike Whole-Class Core Books these arc individually chosen by design).

2.3 where possible and appropriate, the one which does not violate the norms outlined in 1.4 above; in particular, the teacher should be careful to supply and promote novels which, if they be controversial. be so within the *acceptable* canons of 1.4. In short, it is only novels obtained *outside of* class and school that ought to raise serious problems. In such cases, the teacher's role is to mediate and to explain publicly the purposes of this part of the English programme.

B – Safeguards for Student and Teacher In

Dealing With Powerful Literary Texts In

Grades 7-10

3. The Teacher

3.1 The teacher has a duty to press for student engagement with the text in a reasonable manner; through such means as:

– reading or presenting the text in a dramatic manner

– using professional recordings to 'impress' the text

– setting interpretative tasks clearly related to the text and its 'issues', and calling for oral and written responses

– prompting personal responses orally in class or in written form in a journal

– arranging fur appropriate interpretative or personal-response tasks to he discussed in small groups

– demanding sustained attention to the text through reflective re-reading out of class and by compelling students to reach their own consensus about the meaning and value of the text, its themes and its value positions.

3.2 Conversely, the teacher has a duty to protect the privacy, ethical sensibility and self-esteem of individual students within the context of 3.1 above. This may he achieved by such means as:

– ensuring that prompted personal responses in journals arc kept as a private matter between teacher and student (prompted or un-prompted responses will never he 'read aloud' in class without the student's permission)

– arranging for group-discussion tasks-where personal response, opinion or commentary is involved-to be reasonably open-ended

— mediating and modelling appropriate behaviour in group discussion (reciprocity, mutual respect, cooperativeness)

— encouraging individual dissent and personal adjudication of specific value positions implied in the text (the ambiguity of the text should assist here, but teachers must be careful not to signify or impose their views on students)

— allowing a student, on specific occasions, to 'opt for silence' (while encouraging or pressing response over the long term; this is a delicate balancing act)

4. The Student

4.1 The student has an *obligation* to:

— read, reflect upon and respond (freely) to the text

— answer diligently all questions related to the text which do not demand an

 unwarranted personal 'opinion'

— participate as best as he or she can in group talk and whole-class discussion

— offer the sustained attention demanded by complex literary texts

— respond in a journal to teacher-prompts

4.2 The student has a *right* to:

— 'opt for silence' on occasion (even where the question is appropriate)

— reasonable privacy in regard to journal entries

— reasonable dissent regarding the ethical issues raised in texts, presented by peers, *et al.*

— select personal reading material within the accepted norms (sec 2.1 and 1.4)

C. Implementation Strategies

5. School Level

5.1 The principles and safeguards established *in A and B* will require some set procedures at the school and board level if they are to be effective.

5.2 In grades 7 and 8 (where the elementary school has no subject departmental structure). principals should establish among their senior Language Arts staff a *Text Selection and Approval Committee* which shall:

— make decisions on major literary works to he used under the proposed criteria and in light of the particularities of their students, the grade 7-8 English programme as a whole, and, where feasible, the English programme in grades 9 and 10 of the local high school

— outline the teaching methods to be used that will involve students in aspects of personal response, controversial discussion. compulsory group work-and carefully review their obligations and the students' rights

— where possible, review the assignments for response situations to ensure that they are relevant to the study of the text and. where they are interpretative, that they allow for reasonable open-endedness

— assign the task of preparing in written form all the major *kinds of questions* to be raised during the study of the text (including discussion questions, formal writing tasks, and journal prompts); these can be examples only since teachers will need autonomy to adapt and extend.

— meet periodically with the local high-school English teachers to monitor the 7-12/0AC programme for the sort of 'breadth' features mandated in *I-S English: 1987:* i.e., over the course of six years, students in general, should be exposed to a variety of genres, periods, national literatures and literary modes—with attention to multicul-turalism, adult role models, social issues and themes. The latter criteria should not *under any circumstances* be used to select or balance work over a term or a course. The first-order goals must he served before this ·longer-term monitoring be set in motion.

— establish in-school procedures for selecting and displaying personal reading material

— establish procedures for dealing with individual cases of inappropiate selections by students (these could also be set by the Board)

5.3 In high schools with departmental structure the Head of English

should establish subcommittees, as above, to deal with programmes and/or grade divisions. The procedures will he similar to those above except that liaison will be made down to the grade 7-8 feeder school.

6. Board Level

6.1 The role of the board through its administration should not involve the actual selection of specific texts. Nor should the board establish a district-wide panel of experts to do advance screening since many texts-even under the rigid criteria developed here-need lo he assessed in the context of an individual school, class and programme: moreover, since disclosure by the teachers of all major kinds of 'questions' and 'tasks' related to the text is part of the ongoing process the school or department is the best place for the actual selection to he made, rejected after trial, or altered in terms of the tasks set for it.

6.2 Instead, boards, through their administrations, ought to do three

general things:

– initiate meetings and workshops to discuss the guidelines and procedures so that they are firmly grounded

– establish, where appropriate, uniform procedures for dealing with individual crisis situations at the school level

– set up a review committee of English teachers and administrators to deal with serious 'general' challenges to decisions made at the school level

Endnotes

1. The best succinct argument for a content/discipline- based approach to critical thinking is made by McPeek (1981); see in particular chs. 1 and 6.

2. Frank Smith 's notion of the teacher as author's surrogate is discussed fully in (Gutteridge (1983, pp . 31-32).

3. For a recent discussion of public issues in the Canadian high school-with appropriate guidelines for the classroom-sec Werner and Nixon (1990).

4. For a recent and detailed argument against the application of general skills and faculty psychology to curriculum issues, see Barrow (1990).

References

– Barrow. R. (1990). *Understanding Skills: Thinking. Feeling and Caring.* London. ON : The Althouse Press.

– Gutteridge. D. (1983). *Brave Season: Reading and the Language Arts in Grades Seven to Ten.* London. ON: The Althouse Press.

– McPeek. J. (1981). *Critical Thinking and Education* . London. UK: Martin Robertson. Ontario Ministry of Education (1987). *Intermediate-Senior English.* Toronto.

– Werner. W. and Nixon. K. (1979). *The Media and Public Issues: A Guide For Teaching Critical Mindedness.* London, ON: The Althouse Press.

– 02 –

Teaching Literature for Cognitive Development: A Double Perspective

Since 1961 English teachers in Ontario have taught literature and its attendant language skills to two broad streams of students variously labelled five-year *I* four-year, academic *I* non-academic, advanced *I* general, and other less flattering nominations. Excluding the gifted and the learning-disabled—small groups at either end of the continuum—we seem to have accepted the notion that when it comes to understanding literature, and talking and writing about it, there are two classes of students. One class is somehow ' brighter' than the other, is able to read and write with more 'depth.' The second class are not really very good readers: they seem to need lots of help with both comprehension and follow-up writing. Few of us have really believed that these 'general-level' students are capable of any sophisticated form of response to great literary works or that they are able to write about them in sustained and conventionally respectable prose. To substantiate this despairing conclusion one need only glance at the disparity in book titles across the two programs: *Great Expectations* or *The Stone Angel* for the academics and *Jaws* or *I Never Promised You a Rose Garden* for the generals.

Two questions are seldom raised in connection with our attempts to teach literature to various ' levels'. (I) Although any random group of students of the same age is likely to vary markedly in regard to their abilities and behaviours, is it nevertheless possible that two broad streams of student-readers *do* actually exist outside of the extrinsically imposed Robarts' scheme, offering to us two sets of characteristics which are amenable to description, discrimination, and pedagogical application? (2) If so, and if the two sets are critically discrete (not just 'brighter' or' slower'), then are we as teachers looking at two categories representative not merely of differing competencies and achievements but of differing modes of language learning itself? I believe the answer to both questions is yes. Walter Laban's study, a major longitudinal analysis of a whole range of language competencies, suggests that as early as grade one, students can be sorted and ranked, and their future language development confidently predicted (Loban, 1976, ch. 5). Loban monitored 211 students as they moved from kindergarten to grade twelve; using a high group, control group and low group—based on an initial sorting—he noted that the low group reached, in grade five, the same levels in reading, speaking, writing, etc., that the high group had already achieved at the end of grade one. Further, the low group, after twelve years of schooling, had achieved only the grade-nine performance levels of the high group. In short, the former started out about four years behind the latter and remained so throughout their public schooling. Lest we despair, however, it should be pointed out that *all* students continued to learn. It is even conceivable that, if special accommodation were made for the low group throughout the twelve years, the gap could be closed to some degree. (Laban' s study makes no reference to teaching styles or programs.)

In general, all teachers have to face the fact that in a typical unstreamed class student abilities will vary as much as five grades across the *whole spectrum of language skills*. In Ontario by grade nine, this anomaly is recognized officially and students are streamed into two classes (or more). The divisions are formed usually by taking teachers' marks and students' scores on standardized tests, scaling them. and drawing a line about halfway down the column. Having thus created two groups of students, have we then taken advantage of them by designing separate programs? Not very often, and mostly on paper. It is not unfair to conclude that most teachers present the general stream with a "watered down" academic course—substituting 'easier' novels, slowing down the pace, breaking the learning down into smaller units, and giving more direct instruction in grammar, usage, and composition. It has not occurred to us that these students might well respond to fine literature as deeply in some respects as academic students, that there may be forms of writing and expression more suited to their learning style and stage of development. We have been conditioned to think, and casual observation confirms, that academic students can, with their superior vocabulary and control of syntax, understand the 'hard' aspects of reading and writing—those cognitive elements and layers of abstraction we associate, rightly or wrongly, with intelligence. Set against its standard, the general student does not measure up: he or she needs constant supervision and intervention to read and write at all, and rarely, it seems, gets much closer to the so-called cognitive norms of the upper stream.

In response to this somewhat jaded view, a number of experimental programs, here and elsewhere, have attempted to redress the injustices inherent in it (Fidler, 1969; Dixon, 1979; Medway, 1980; Holt, 1964). Typically, these experimental approaches assume, in an attempt to correct past imbalances, that general students are somehow more 'emotional,' 'tuned in to life,' 'realistic,' 'experience-oriented,' even more 'honest' than their academic counterparts who are 'scholarly,' 'detached,' and 'cerebral.' In the past ten years we have seen a proliferation of humanities and integrated courses (Underhill and Telford, 1978) and the promotion of learning theories extrapolated from them (Medway, Holt, Dixon). In Ontario, we have had a run at media, film, man-in-society, life-themes, and so on, many of which have proved very successful. Indeed, it is the success of some of these experiments which compels us to raise the issue of whether or not there *are* genuine differences-in needs, skills, contents, and *learning styles between* the two large streams we have created. However, the simple explanation of these success stories that great literature and cognitive goals should be replaced by relevant texts and experiential objectives will not do. It patronizes and demeans both groups. It says to the general student that he or she has feelings and ideas but that these are limited to less-than-first-rate literature and tied to a narrow band of egocentric experience. On the other hand, it implies that academic students use their advanced linguistic strategies to keep poetry at a safe distance, to critique more than respond, or to set up worlds apart from the quotidian. These are dangerous half-truths. The academic and general student, if they exist, cannot usefully be distinguished along scales of emotionality, worldliness or egocentricity.

If there are useful ways of categorizing students as readers and writers, what are they? And how can we take pedagogical advantage of them? The answer lies partly in the nature of reading and writing. *Both are essentially cognitive processes.* Comprehending a literary text—and getting the meaning by whatever means—is, as Frank Smith has noted (1978, ch. 5), a mental operation; and no tampering with the mechanics will ever change that. We read with our minds; and if our comprehension strategies broaden and deepen so that we can read more complex and varied texts, it is because we are using our minds more efficiently. We have, *ipso facto,* acquired cognitive skills, even though we might find it hard to pin down specific subskills or sketch the precise sequence of learning events. Reading, then, whether it be of a novel or a late-slip, does not *in essence* vary. That is the message so stunningly delivered to us by psycholinguists over the last decade and demonstrated so convincingly in school programs like those developed by James Moffett (Moffett and Wagner, 1976) and Don Holdaway (1979). Though other factors impinge, comprehension *is* fundamentally cognitive. In this strict sense then, there can be only one type of reader: an individual with his mind set on getting meaning from a printed text.

Having said that, however, we must turn away from the text and the reader's 'decoding' problems and look at the *contextual strategies* which Smith has enumerated and which have been incorporated into the Moffett and Holdaway experiments. Here we may see some marked differences in reading behaviour. The reader does not confront a text in a vacuum. Texts can be read silently, aloud, or be presented by a skilled reader; their topics can be discussed beforehand; each reader brings along his or her own experience and world-picture as well as their previous exposure to aspects of discourse; one text can prepare for and illuminate the next; the patterns of a text and their *predictive* potential, when presented dynamically by the teacher, can substantively affect the decoding of that text and future texts with similar structures. All these contexts: prior knowledge, setting, and presentational format have been shown empirically to be better determinants of so-called readability levels than vocabulary control and word-frequency (Smith, 1978a, pp. 230-234). In fact, it is fair to conclude that prior knowledge (a context factor) and predictive patterning (text factor), along with the inherent interest of a text for the reader (psychological factor), are the primary requisites for successful comprehension.

Holdaway demonstrated the effect of patterned texts with strong psychological impact on primary school children *vis a vis* the weak or arbitrary patterning of graded readers with their well-laundered stories. It is clear from his experiments that reading improves for all children only when exceptional literature—classic poems and stories rhetorically rich and psychologically powerful—is used and presented in the most dramatic way possible. The consequent carryover into writing and other symbolizing activities is marvelously illustrated (ch. 7), and heartening. Around such literary texts is woven a skein of dramatic, visual, mimetic, and expressive activities which set up in turn a context of prior knowledge for ensuing reading encounters.

What has this approach to primary reading got to do with teaching literature to intermediate and senior students? It presents us with a valid theory of how children best learn to read initially. Part of that theory says that literature set in a highly controlled context increases comprehension levels, promotes the acquisition of a variety of reading strategies (beyond phonics and word-by-word decoding), and hence advances those cognitive skills related to reading-as-a-mental-process; that is, prediction and interpretation based on the sorting, categorizing, and application of previously experienced linguistic structures to novel texts. This may sound too complex for a six-year-old, but even though we cannot label the individual parts of the process, we are pretty sure that some such set of mental operations underlies all reading comprehension. And almost all six-year-olds *can* be taught to read, particularly if the Smith/Holdaway approach is used. But why, after initial reading is established, are some readers better than others, even by the end of grade one? And why do the discrepancies continue throughout schooling to the point where, by the time students reach high school, they present to us not only a wide range of 'test scores' but two distinct sets of reading behaviours? While no one knows the answer to this question, it seems from the available evidence (Loban, 1976; Dixon, 1979; Holdaway, 1979) that children who start school with deficits in the contextual area—book behaviour, speech base, knowledge of the world—get off to a slow start and rarely recover. Holdaway's program in New Zealand attempted to compensate for these deficits, with some success, but the students who arrived in school with a well-developed 'literacy set' (p. 62), did make the predictable gains. Indeed, they profited even more from a program designed to continue and deepen the pattern of learning they brought with them from home. Of the two crucial elements in comprehension—context and predictiveness of text—a paucity of contextual experience before the years of schooling begin seems severely to impede the progress of any student. However, emphasizing context and the selection of powerful literary texts did prove beneficial to *all students,* though to varying degrees.

Hence, the *advanced* reader and what we will call the *normal* reader appear to proceed along diverging paths once the initial phase of reading is complete, and the critical difference in the behaviour of the two classes lies in *the relative dependency of each group upon the context and presentational setting of the text.* By the time they reach the intermediate division, normal and advanced readers are becoming distinguishable in their achievement, behaviour, and pedagogical dependencies.

What the intermediate-senior teacher of English needs to recognize is that while reading comprehension remains fundamentally a cognitive process, the context in which it occurs can and ought to vary for the normal and advanced reader. Advanced readers begin to mark themselves off from normal readers by demanding less and less of the contextual aspects of reading (though never fully abandoning them); and are becoming more independent of the immediate language situation and, thus, correspondingly more skilled at comprehending texts as texts; that is, as isolated linguistic structures which they can decode (often in very novel circumstances) and compare with other related textual structures from past experience, and begin to create categories (genres) and deploy them in further predictive strategems. This process starts very early, manifests itself strongly with the onset of self-conscious behaviour (around age eleven or so, though gifted children display it much earlier), and develops throughout high school.

The normal reader, in contrast, remains bound and vulnerable to the immediate language situation. He or she comprehends best when the text is presented in a dynamic, rather than reflective, manner and when it has been carefully programmed to match his prior experience of the world and of closely allied complementary texts. Comprehension diminishes when texts are put to students with no preparation or prior framework of connections (themes, plot-lines, moral and social issues). The so-called readability formulas which rely on word frequency and syntactical complexity only come into play in a meaningful way when the text is indeed isolated. But it rarely is, for even the normal reader will have access to much *implicit* cognitive knowledge (from prior reading experience) needed to get meaning-from-text; however, it will have to be activated, stimulated, or evoked from the outside, from the context. The normal reader, in short, often needs not more direct instruction about 'tactics with the text' but rather constant motivation, a highly-charged language environment, and a guiding adult to design appropriate settings that will incite the reader to *use* the resource base he or she already possesses but has trouble calling into conscious application. Like the advanced reader, the normal one will also need first-rate literature with powerful predictive values; this factor, related as it is intrinsically to the text and to human nature, remains constant for all readers at all levels.

Put. another way, the advanced reader appropriates the knowledge of linguistic structures from literary texts so thoroughly and cumulatively that they eventually become an *autonomous instrument* with which to think, to feel, and to express. Normal readers, though somewhat less reliant on context as he matures, still operate best when a text remains undetached from its psychological/cultural/moral setting, which usually means that it is close to their own concerns and interests. While their response may be as emotional as any other readers; and their ability to discuss themes and moral issues second to none, they rarely come to see texts and their special linguistic potential as autonomous. For them, language serves in its setting: to help one feel, present opinions, and look at the world with more objectivity. They call on it when they need to. That is why I prefer to call him or her with no condescension whatsoever, the *normal* reader and user of language: This is the way most of us use our speaking and writing skills, or the reason we buy a book, see a movie, or discuss the latest TV serial with friends. We recruit language and its inherent cognitive elements into the service of reading and expressing in *immediate situations* and for *demonstrable purposes*. The instrumentality of language *per se* remains invisible. If our daily lives continue to be enriched by reading, viewing, and friendly discussion, then the instrument will continue to evolve without, in most instances, becoming any more visible.

As high school English teachers we ought to be aware, then, that we are dealing with two modes of learning for what is a common mental process. Advanced readers, whether we intercede or not, will become self-conscious readers and writers, and they comprehend best when working from context-to-text or text-within-a-context.. Figure I illustrates this contrast in learning styles:

In each case, growth in comprehension ability (both acquired strategies and measurable achievement) will increase as long as the respective learning needs are

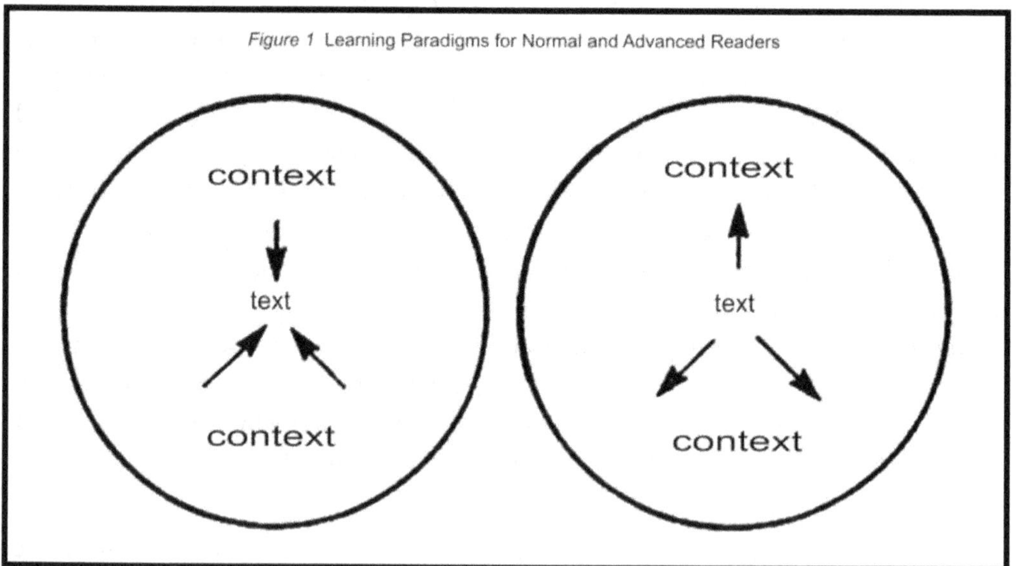

accommodated. As Figure 2 indicates, some 'normal; readers may well turn into 'advanced' ones as maturation patterns and effective pedagogy take over.

Nevertheless, we should not be setting, as program objectives, goals which purport to change all normal readers into advanced ones. Though a contradiction in terms. this

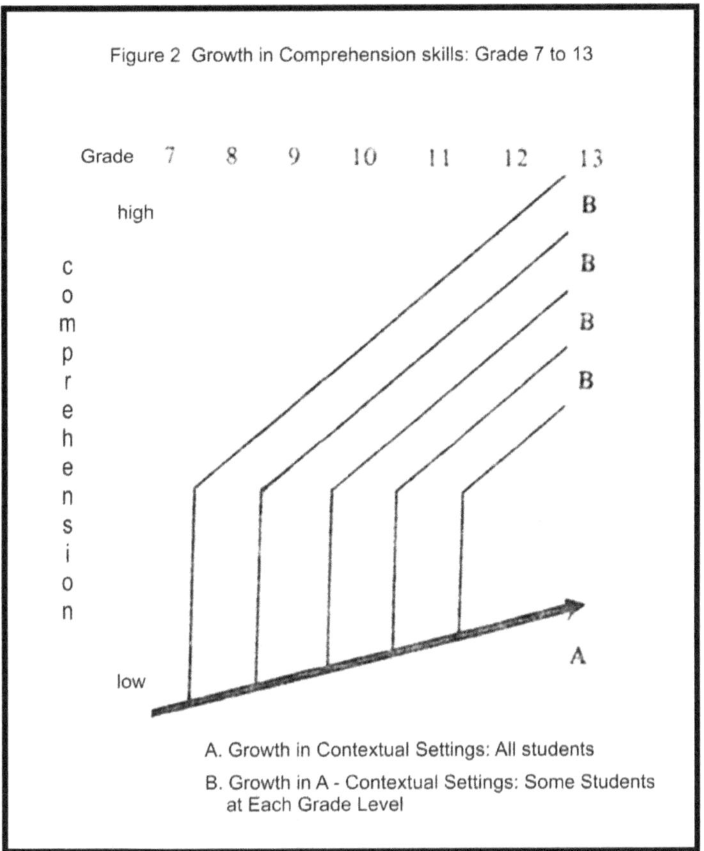

approach appears to underlie twenty years of our 'watering down' academic courses to a variety of 'levels.'

We have, then, the rudimentary outlines of a learning framework appropriate to intermediate-senior students. It has a double perspective but a common line of cognitive development and as all students improve year to year as readers; they will, relative to their ability and learning style, be able to comprehend more complex and varied texts; and they will learn the uses and pleasures of literature—moral, cultural, and psychological—as they progress. In this sense there is no essential difference in the program goals for the two groups, though as we have seen, performance levels will always vary. A difference emerges only when we *add to* the advanced reading program the need for autonomy, which in turn will result in extended and special uses for literature not fully available to normal readers: the capacity to internalize large linguistic structures and deploy them at will in the decoding of novel texts in isolation, to create imaginative frameworks derived from a series of texts alone, and to apply these as metaphorical instruments to the interpretation of experience. The normal reader, of course, will be able to do some of these operations, but not without a context provided by the teacher and his or her course design, and then only in an implicit way.

If the foregoing hypothesis has any validity, it could have the following effects on how we think about our English programs in grades seven to twelve.

1. Students, as readers, will no longer be classified according to oversimplified experiential, moral, or intelligence norms.

2. Students will gradually *sort themselves out* as normal or advanced principally in terms of their behaviour *vis a vis* texts—autonomous or contextual, neither learning style being intrinsically 'better' than the other.

3. All students will be exposed to all the usual pleasures and uses of good literature—psychological, cultural and moral—without prejudice.

4. The best literature appropriate to age and learning style will be used because of its predictive patterning and psychological attraction. While *Wuthering Heights* may be inappropriate for a normal grade twelve, *The Old Man and the Sea,* set in a proper context, is not. Conversely, advanced twelves should never be given a novel inappropriate to their moral/psychological/cultural needs just because 'it'll stretch their minds' or 'get them ready for university.' Both sets of readers have *inalienable cognitive and experiential rights.*

5. The fallacy of multiple streaming (based on scaling students' comprehension scores and/or teachers' marks) is clearly exposed. Since only two learning styles are required to promote growth in comprehension, *no more than two streams will ever be needed.* (An exception might occur for 'non-readers' and the learning disabled for whom, in any case, special arrangements are customarily made.)

6. While a student who performs best in a contextual setting will have his or her learning severely impaired by premature exposure to the demands of an autonomous style ('watered-down academic'), the converse is not necessarily true. The advanced reader, if given opportunities for independent study, will be able to function comfortably in a course designed along contextual lines, at least in the early stages of any advancement.

7. Hence, *most courses in the intermediate division* (grades seven to ten), where many emergent autonomous readers are revealed, *ought to be mainly contextual in design.* Only the most clearly-marked advanced students should be streamed out so that they may have the special benefits of the paradigm more suited to them. In terms of the stages outlined in the Ontario Ministry of Education *Intermediate English* guideline (1977, pp. 28-35), this means advanced stage III and all stage IV readers. Nothing is gained by erring on the side of premature advancement. Autonomous readers in a flexible contextual program will sort themselves out by their behaviour and perfomance.

8. Evaluation in comprehension should be made, for all students, in both contextual settings (tests/presentations at the end of units where the teacher's design and direction have materially assisted comprehension) and in acontextual ones, some of which will be

severely acontextual (norm-referenced tests, OAIP items, sight texts on arbitrarily-timed exams) and others only partly so (sight passages very similar to ones just reviewed in context, independent study of a novel related to an ongoing unit, *etc.*). It is just as important to know what skills have been learned and what achievements attained by a student for whom all the non-textual factors have been heightened as it is to know what he will do with a text dropped with chilly randomness on his desk. As teachers we need to know what each student can do in each circumstance. There are different applications of intelligence operating here which in the real world will serve their separate ends. *To suggest that any student's reading ability be measured only by the least contextually contaminated test,* given what we are now learning about language learning, is *educationally fallacious and morally perverse.* We may have to learn to live with the relativity of assessment that says, 'given this kind of book on that sort of occasion, student X can see plot design, explicate certain themes, relate these to his own experience, *etc.*'. This mode may well be less functional in a purely 'academic' system, but it is surely more valid and infinitely more humane.

9. When the need for distinct courses or programs is appropriate, every facet of pedagogy, text selection, unit planning, methods, evaluation, will be deployed deliberately to reflect the differing learning styles of normal and advanced readers.

10. In very general terms, a course/program tailored to contextual learning would:

    – present high-quality literature to students in a dynamic manner: oral reading, dramatization, guided discussion.

    – provide complementary texts and experience, thematic and linguistic, to increase prior knowledge: related books, films, discussion of current events, newspaper and magazine articles.

    – stress the thematic/experiential outcomes of reading texts, and evaluate through these outcomes rather than through the teaching and analysis of subskills

    – build discussion, writing, and other expressive activities out of the reading to keep the focus on function rather than form

    – encourage independent reading of books around the core materials to reinforce acquired competencies and stress the uses and pleasures of literature

11. In very general terms, a course/program tailored to an autonomous learning style, while not excluding many of the contextual elements of the other program, would:

    – present texts in a way that encourages reflective reading and response, deepened by analysis and extension into thematic discussion, and the building up of world-pictures and frameworks for interpreting experience.

    – organize the literature to promote text-by-text comparison, thematic and generic,- with opportunity for independent response to novel examples

    – encourage independent reading and writing on self-initiated topics

– evaluate all aspects of the above through response to sight passages, written essays, and the monitoring of group discussion.

The pedagogical demands implicit in the foregoing are indeed imposing, even awesome (see Gutteridge 1978 and 1981 for some detailed suggestions). But methodology has always been a secondary procedure, subsequent to the setting of goals, which in turn are only of value when they reflect what students can actually achieve. Both goals and methods, then, are constrained by the inevitable learning curve of the children we teach, a curve we are at last beginning to understand. In reading, and in language learning in general, we do know we are up against complex cognitive processes so intricate they will never be fully explicated. Nevertheless, recognizing the centrality of the cognitive and getting over our prejudices about the apparent incompatibility of 'domains'—cognitive/affective, scholarly/real, academic/experiential, bright/slow—represent significant steps forward. If we can come to accept—not out of pity, guilt, political motive, or personal need—that all our students can and do become better readers each day of their lives; that any such reading gains are essentially cognitive; that however they are attained (autonomously or contextually, alone or with lots of help), they represent genuine learning achievements. And accept also that for most of our students the normal and lifelong pattern of reading will be constrained and enlivened by context; and that we ought to accept that 'limitation' with good grace. If we do, then the difficulties of matching pedagogy and program will seem, in the long view, insubstantial. On the other hand, without some guiding hypothesis—however tentative—of how students actually learn to read, the task will be impossible.

References

Dixon, John. *Education 1~19: The Role of English and Communication,* London: Macmillan, 1979.

Fidler, Barbara. 'A Teacher's Experience with the Ontario Pilot Project in English,' *The English Quarterly,* I, I (Summer 1968), pp. 91-93.

Gutteridge, Don. *The Country of the Young: Units in Canadian Literature For Elementary and Secondary School,* London, Ontario: Faculty of Education, U. W.O., 1978.

'Teaching Canadian Literature: A Cultural Odyssey,' *Indirections,* VI, 2 (Spring 1981), pp. 22-27.

Holdaway, Don. *The Foundations of Literacy,* New York: Scholastic, 1979.

Holt, John. *How Children Fail,* New York: Dell, 1964.

Loban, Walter. *Language Development: Kindergarten Through Grade Twelve,* Urbana, Illinois: N.C.T.E., 1976.

Medway, Peter. *Finding a Language: Autonomy and Learning in School,* Richmond Surrey, England: Writers' and Readers' Coop, 1980.

Moffett, James and Wagner, Betty Jane. *Student-Centred Language Arts and Reading, K-13,* 2nd ed., Boston: Houghton-Mifflin, 1976.

Ontario Ministry of Education. *English: Intermediate Division* (guideline), Toronto: 1977.

Ontario Ministry of Education. *Ontario Assessment Instrument Pool: Intermediate English I* and *Intermediate English II,* Toronto: 1981.

Smith, Frank. *Reading Without Nonsense,* New York: Teachers' College Press, 1978.

Smith, Frank. *Understanding Reading,* 2nd ed., New York: Holt, Rinehart and Winston, 1978(a).

Underhill, Ian and Telford, Peter. *Integrated Studies,* London, Ontario: London Board of Education, 1978.

– 03 –

Shakespeare by Ear:

Macbeth Through Listening and Discussion

Not the least of the many problems associated with teaching Shakespearean tragedy to senior high school students is the fact that many of our seventeen and eighteen year-olds simply have not acquired sufficient rhetorical skill to read the plays—even at the literal or basic comprehension level. Much progress has been made in recent years, especially in the use of visual aids like films, T.V. tapes, filmstrips *et. al.* Some progress has even been achieved in the area of creative drama. Still, there remains the difficulty of Shakespeare's language, and the feeling that we are hedging, are circumventing the poetry by, as McLuhan might say, 'hotting up' the visual and motor dimensions (spectacle, movement, gesture, *etc.*) in the desperate belief that somehow the language will be understood, or at least accepted. One is quick to note that these approaches are unquestionably superior to the usual alternatives: analyzing the play laboriously for eight weeks, or not teaching Shakespeare at all.

The program of study and methodology outlined below can provide us with yet another alternative, one which meets Shakespeare's text straight on while avoiding the sterility of analytical methods and the dangers of overstressing visuality, ('the despotism of the eye' Coleridge calls it). Not the eye nor the body moving, but the ear: listening is a more certain way into the poetry and drama of Shakespeare. The aural faculty, like the sense of smell, is more synthetic than we often imagine, and may be the best way in, and then out towards spectacle, movement, rhythm—the total drama and its nexus with experience. Listening, and then talk, as well, mediating the experience received and the experience expressed a middle ground between analysis and the frozen speech of the written word.

Rationale:

This unit is designed for those students aged seventeen to eighteen who have not yet acquired enough rhetorical reading skills to cope with a textual analysis approach to a major Shakespearean play. The unit is predicated upon the following assumptions: that these students (1) are mature enough to respond to the experiential (affective) dimensions of the play; (2) are capable of understanding the language through *gestalt* reactions as opposed to an analytical response, so long as it is received in its 'dramatic context and in complete or 'whole' units (subscenes, scenes, acts); (3) have had some previous training in operating their own discussion groups.

The ideal dramatic context, of course, is to have each class see a live production of the play. Since this is a practical impossibility in most schools, teachers have been compelled to find approximate dramatic contexts; *viz.*, acting out scenes on stage or in the classroom; viewing films of the play in part or in whole; listening to records, *etc.* While the following method incorporates all of these approaches, it focusses chiefly on listening. The advantages of this focus are four-fold: (1) it allows the power of Shakespeare's poetry to be heard and apprehended in the *gestalt* manner of all great poetry without, for the moment, the initial distractions occasioned by the visual components of film; (2) listening, as a first-experience, allows the imagination of the student to operate fully: it compels him to listen to *voices*, to their special characteristics, their interaction, and to begin the process of translating them into rich visual terms—without the intermediate step of reading/analysis and without the intimidation of a filmic presentation, which, for students who lack rhetorical skills in general and are naturally drawn to the literal reading of experience, can be overpowering and ultimately reductive; (3) it follows from (1) and (2) that listening as a first-experience is more compatible with parallel reading than a full visual presentation might be; in short, we want the students to find it a natural process to move from an initial listening experience to a re-'reading'; or more properly: listening, talking, re-'reading'; (4) while it is possible, and perhaps even desirable, to begin with the students' acting out various scenes and then work back into the text and its implications for character, feeling and theme, such a procedure is very difficult for many English teachers to effect, and doubly difficult with older students with little or no previous training in dramatics. Listening, on the other hand, is the more 'natural' and certainly the more pragmatic prelude to talk, and talk more readily leads to re-reading and further discussion—even to writing, although that is not a central concern here.

Goals:

In exposing 'non-academic' (supply your own euphemism) students to Shakespeare, we must needs reduce many of our cherished academic aims, especially in the cognitive domain. However, there may well be a corresponding expansion of the experiential and affective areas. Indeed, some of the cognitive goals may be implicitly achieved *en route*; *e.g.*, image patterns and dramatic 'structure'.

Here are the general and primary goals:

(1) to have students experience through the characters and their conflicts the central issues of the play.

(2) to have students feel the central concerns of the play and respond to them—their own personal experience.

(3) to have students discuss these concerns and their feelings with one another in a spontaneous and open manner.

(4) to have students gain enough interest and confidence to want to see the play performed or to view several film versions and discuss their reaction.

(5) to improve the following skills:
> (a) listening
> (b) visualizing
> (c) reading dramatic literature in its various contexts
> (d) discussion

From these general goals, specific aims may be formulated for the particular play(s) to be studied. In the example given below (*Macbeth*) the specific goals are implied throughout the question sequences.

Secondary goals might include:

(1) to have students feel the power of language and imagery in revealing character, conflict, moral dilemmas, *etc.*

(2) to have students read or see or listen—willingly—to other Shakespearean plays.

(3) to have students begin a discussion of what 'tragedy' involves (in its affective sense}, with a view to exploring the phenomenon in other plays, novels, films, *etc.*

Procedures:

Phase I: The Play as a Whole

(1) Select a suitable recording of the whole play. Since the aim of this phase is to have the students respond in a *gestalt* manner to an uninterrupted aural presentation of the text, it is advisable to select a recording which has a great deal of dramatic power, including appropriate sound effects and musical accompaniment where necessary, even though many of the best recordings of this type are often 'incomplete' renderings of the full text. Since the students will not be following the script in their books at this stage, dramatic power should take precedence over completeness. A superior recording as textually complete as possible is, of course, the ideal.

(2) Play the recording right through, if possible, or play it over the course of two or three periods. Students will not use their texts, though they may have them in their possession at this time (some students may, even at this early stage, begin to read or browse through the script after class). When the 'performance' has been completed, begin a forty or fifty-minute discussion of their responses and reactions.

(3) Direct their responses only in the most general way, since this phase should be as free and open-ended as possible. Use natural questions like "What sort of people is this play about?" "What kind of problems did they have?" "What happened to this one or that one?" "What did you feel near the end of the play?" "Who did you admire in the play? Dislike?" "When did all of this happen?" Do not attempt to clarify invalid or even incorrect responses; we want their first and frank reactions. When obvious disagreements arise ('I felt sorry for Lady Macbeth'/'I thought she was a witch') note the area of conflict on a special place on the blackboard, under the heading 'Questions and Problems'. If and when certain responses are repeated, or motif words are mentioned in the natural flow of talk (guilt, murder, regret, *etc.*), merely jot them down as items to be explored. Keep the 'Questions and Problems' section permanently on the blackboard throughout the detailed study of the play—or, where this is not feasible, make up a ditto sheet recording these first impressions in summary form. Do not let the students know, in any way, where you stand on any of the questions or problems raised; be scrupulous about using *their* motif words (even though 'remorse' may be more useful than 'kept feeling sorry'). Eliciting first impressions from a *gestalt* response can only be accomplished in an open and democratic atmosphere.

(4) Inform the students that you now intend to take them on a more leisurely tour through the play in order to answer the questions raised, to resolve conflicting responses where possible, and to broaden and deepen their understanding of the issues in the play. They will be *listening* to the play again, and will have a chance to air their views in the discussion-groups. Tell them that they may, if they wish, begin reading the play on their own time. A relatively unannotated text (Penguin or Pelican series) is best, since elaborate foot-notes are useful only for an analytical approach. However, very brief textual notes may serve to aid a private reading so long as they do not slow it down too much. Again, speed, *gestalt* reactions and context are the best hope for comprehension by students with limited rhetorical skills.

Phase II: Listening, Talking, Reading

This phase is a natural progression from Phase I; the mode of presentation has not changed—they are still listening—but the *gestalt* units are now shorter and will be experienced sequentially, with some talk set between units. Their first impressions can be explored and modified, influenced now by a parallel reading of the text and by more time for reflection and structured by the sequential logic of the drama itself.

(1) Using questions like those below (designed for *Macbeth*), play a scene or short group of scenes—12-15 minutes is ideal and have the students listen and follow the script. Take 5-10 minutes, no more, to discuss the questions with them. You should give out all the listening questions at the beginning of Phase II. Students should be encouraged but not compelled to read ahead with the relevant questions in mind.

(2) At the conclusion of each listening unit, the questions should be taken up briskly. Whenever disagreements arise, explore them briefly, and where possible with reference to the text as heard; if students spontaneously refer to the printed text, reinforce their actions, of course. But do not use the printed text yourself as a means of directing the discussion except for the brief underlining exercises in some questions. We are still in a modified *gestalt* situation, where impressions, while more structured, are still more significant than considered reflections gained through analysis. The procedure, essentially, is a brisk, run-through the questions, which, you will notice, are keyed to aural responses. Variant responses can again be handled easily by referring to the 'Problems and Questions' outline—let them go unanswered or unsolved because there will still be time to explore them in Phase III. In Phase II pacing is all-important since we are still trying

to have them experience the power of this play as heard while adding the dimension of talk and some parallel and/or preparatory reading. How long to spend on a scene and its questions, or how to group the scenes to achieve a reasonable rhythm in your lesson sequences, must be left to the discretion and agility of the teacher. However, if the aims of Phase II are kept clearly in view, and if the 'Questions and Problems' outline is used to focus discussion and provide a cumulative commentary on the progress of the class through the play, the pacing should take care of itself.

(3) By the end of Phase II the following issues and aspects of the play should be clarified, though not likely resolved:

- the development of the plot(s)

- the basic nature of the main characters (with much ambiguity still to be resolved)

- the basic conflicts (leaving much complexity to be explored)

- the emotional rhythm or movement of the play

- the moral questions (in need of further study and discussion)

- some of the significant and dramatically obvious images

- the secondary problems associated with the time of the play, its historical context, anachronisms, and some if its 'probable impossibilities'

Listening Questions For Phase II: Macbeth

The following features of these questions should be noted:

(1) Many of them are directed toward aural responses and/or parallel reading exercises like marking phrases, underlining images, *etc.*

(2) In many instances, the questions are set up to frame the students' responses, and thus should be read before the listening begins.

(3) The structuring, and demands, of the questions increases act by act throughout the play, taking into account that student responses are cumulative and that student confidence grows from day to day.

Act One

Scene 1

1. Give two or three adjectives to describe the atmosphere of the scene.

2. What main character is mentioned. What future event?

Scene 2

1. List several actions described to us that reveal Macbeth's heroic qualities.

2. What kind of king does Duncan seem to be? How is he treated by those around him?

3. What reward is given Macbeth at the end of the scene? Why?

Scene 3

1. List phrases that reveal the witches' evil nature, their vengefulness, their super-natural powers.

2. Name the *three* prophecies given to Macbeth and to Banquo.

3. In a phrase for each, show the reaction each has to these prophecies.

4. a) After Ross informs Macbeth of his new appointment, what lines reveal Macbeth's ambition?

   b) What decision does he make regarding his politics, his future?

Scene 4

1. Listen carefully to the speeches of Macbeth and Banquo. Which seem the most sincere? Why?

2. What is Macbeth's reaction to the king's unexpected announcement?

3. Find the irony in Duncan's final speech.

Scene 5

1. a) Mark phrases in Lady Macbeth's opening speeches (11. 1-54) which indicate her determination, her heartlessness, her sense of evil.

   b) How does she view her role in the enterprise at hand?

2. Listen to the sounds and images of her soliloquies. What mood do they create in the listener?

3. What is Macbeth's reaction to his wife's proposal for the murder of Duncan that very night?

Scene 6

1. Listen to the sound and images of the opening speeches. Why is it ironic?

Scene 7

1. a) What reasons does Macbeth offer for not murdering Duncan?

   b) What images suggest Macbeth's sense of guilt? his fear of consequences?

   c) Name the only reason he gives for the murder.

   d) What conclusion does he reach?

2. Listen to Lady Macbeth's arguments to persuade her husband. What two seem most effective? Why?

Act Two

Scene 1

1. Mark the phrases that suggest the darkness of the night (11. 1-10).

2. a) Where is Macbeth going when he meets Banquo?

   b) How does he attempt to cover up?

3. a) What feelings are created in the audience during Macbeth's soliloquy?

   b) What images are suggestive of the murder? of the horror of the deed?

Act Two

Scene 2

1. What details create unbearable tension at the opening of the scene (11. 1-20)?

2. What lines show that Macbeth is fearful? Conscience stricken?

3. What is Lady Macbeth's reaction to her husband's weakness?

4. Listen to the knocking during the scene. What effect does it ·have on the listener?

5. Account for the dramatic power of Macbeth's closing lines.

Scene Three

1. What purposes are served by the Porter's speech (both comic and serious)?

2. (a) How well do Macbeth and his wife disguise their guilty feelings during
   the scene? (Be specific.)

   (b) What errors, if any, do they make?

3. Why do Duncan's sons decide to flee? How will this help Macbeth?

Scene Four

1. Ross and the Old Man discuss "the deed that's done." What strange happenings
   have occurred?

2. What phrases suggest Macduff is suspicious of Macbeth?

3. To what extent has Macbeth's plan worked?

Act Three

Scene 1

1. (a) How is Banquo made the centre of attention at the beginning of the scene?

   (b) What changes in Macbeth's manner do you notice here?

2. Listen carefully to Macbeth's soliloquy:

   (a) What reasons does he give for wanting to kill Banquo?

   (b) Mark the phrases which suggest that Macbeth is suffering from feelings
   of guilt.

(c) Describe the tone of the speech. (Is it rational? excited? calm? *etc.*)

3. How does Macbeth skillfully motivate the Murderers to carry out their task?

Scene 2

1. Listen carefully to the tone and tension of this scene.

   (a) Mark the phrases that reveal Macbeth's fear, his sense of guilt.

   (b) Note the number of images referring to darkness and sleep. Why can't Macbeth sleep?

   (c) What does the darkness mean for Macbeth?

2. Give several proofs to show that Lady Macbeth's control over her husband is slipping.

3. What terrible philosophy does Macbeth utter in the closing lines of the scene?

Scene 3

1. As you listen to this scene, what devices create suspense and a sense of horror?

2. What is the significance of Fleance's escape?

Scene 4

1. What is Macbeth's reaction· to the Murderer's report?

2. What makes Macbeth's discovery of the ghost dramatic?

3. Describe Lady Macbeth's desperate attempts to save the situation.

4. What makes the Ghost's second appearance even more dramatically powerful?

5. This scene marks a turning point in the play.

   (a) To what extent is Macbeth now suspected by the other Lords?

   (b) What evidence is there that his mind is beginning to crack from guilt, that he has chosen an irreversible course of evil?

   (c) What signs suggest that even the close relationship of husband and wife is beginning to widen, to dissolve?

Scene 6

1. Compare the mood of this scene with that of III, 4.

2. List three or four important bits of information given here.

3. What suggests that Macduff, Malcolm and England will play a key role in saving Scotland?

Act Four

Scene 1

1. Give *two* or *three* adjectives to describe the mood of this scene (11. 1-45).

2. ·outline-the *three* warnings given to Macbeth by the witches? ·

3. What symbolic values can you find for the Armed Head, the Bloody Child, the Child Crowned?

4. Briefly describe Macbeth's reactions to *each* of these announcements? to the show of eight kings?

5. Listen carefully to Macbeth's last speech in this scene and then suggest why the audience now knows he is irrevocably doomed?

Scene 2

1. What details create tension at the beginning of the scene?

2. What feelings do you have as you listen to the conversation between Lady Macduff and her young son?

Scene 3

This long scene slows down the action before the excitement and confusion of the last act; it also develops the character of Malcolm and Macduff, the two men who will save Scotland.

1. (a) Why does Malcolm distrust Macduff at first?

   (b) What test does he devise to prove Macduff's loyalty? How does it work?
     (11. l-135)

2. What sort of picture are we given of the State of Scotland?

3. (a) Discuss the dramatic power of Ross' revelation to Macduff.

   (b) On what note does the scene conclude?

Act Five

Scene 1

1. How does the opening conversation between the Doctor and the gentleman create suspense, and prepare us for Lady Macbeth's entrance?

2. What are your feelings as you listen to Lady Macbeth's words in this scene?

3. What significance can you sec in the fact that Lady Macbeth's madness takes the form of sleep-walking, that she cannot wash the blood off her hands?

Scene 2 – 4

1. What picture of Macbeth do the Scottish Lords give us in scene 2?

2. Mark the lines in scene 3 which show Macbeth's desperate faith in the witches, his self-pity, his physical courage.

3. What evidence are we given in scene IV that Macbeth will be defeated?

Scene 5

1. Mark phrases in this scene which suggest:

   – Macbeth's physical courage

   – his deep sense of depression

   – his loss of all normal feeling

2. In one sentence, give the philosophy of life presented in the "tomorrow and tomorrow" soliloquy.

Scene 6 – 9

1. How do the two prophecies of the witches "come true" for Macbeth?

2. What factors might cause us to pity Macbeth? to despise him?

3. Listen to Malcolm's final speech.

    (a) With what feelings does it leave the audience?

    (b) Haw does it provide a fitting conclusion to the play?

Phase III: Discussion and Synthesis

The students now move from the listening/parallel reading phase to one involving an exploration of the larger questions raised by and through the drama. The mode is now mainly talk, structured by a series of teacher questions (though the questions should seem a natural extension of the 'Questions and Problems' outline new fully developed), and a more careful re-reading of key scenes and speeches. Some analysis is necessarily involved but it differs from a straight analytical methodology in these ways: (1) it has been preceded by series of <u>gestalt</u> experiences mediated by teacher-directed talk, giving students an initial grasp of the play and a growing confidence in their ability to comprehend it; (2) it involves some private reading but a great deal of the re-reading will be done in groups where talk is once again a mediating factor; and (3) each unit of analytical work is set in a clearly structured 'frame' derived from the previous context of listening and discussion, and thus seen to be an extension of question, issues and responses raised by .the students themselves. In short·, analysis, or a more detailed reading of key scenes, has at least a three-fold purpose: to clarify, to resolve and to synthesize.

More specifically, students are placed in their customary discussion groups, given the 'Question for Discussion' (see below), and encouraged to carry out their awn further exploration of the play. The teacher might review the 'Questions and Problems' outline before beginning; however, there will be an obvious correlation, sooner or later, between the outline and question sheets handed out.

Group-discussion techniques are complex and cannot be detailed here. But it may be sufficient to mention several important points:

    (1) Students should now be encouraged to read on their own as much as they can, and to prepare for each discussion-group session in advance.

    (2) One or two large questions .should be-attempted in a forty-five minute period.

    (3) Student responses should be largely oral, though a recording secretary for each group might make point-form notes to facilitate follow-up discussion.

    (4) Responses to the Questions For Discussion' should be reviewed by the whole class, with the teacher as chairman where necessary, following each act of the play, or after each question if difficulties have arisen.

(5) The teacher must facilitate the discussion by sitting in with a group from time to time, by circulating about the room in the role of resource person or mediator, by calling the whole class together when the occasion warrants and 'teaching' a quick, intensive ten-minute lesson as a means of redirecting the class, and by keeping up the <u>confidence</u> of the students at all times.

Questions For Discussion: Macbeth

<u>Act One</u>

1. Compare Macbeth as he is seen from the outside (by the people of Scotland) to the view we get of him from inside.

Reference: I, 2

I, 3 (Sol. "Two Truths are told")

I, 4 (Macbeth's aside, 1 148 ff.)

2. Compare the reactions of Banquo and Macbeth to the witches and their prophecies. What do these reactions tell us about the two men? About the <u>real</u> power and control of the witches?

Reference: I, 3

3. Write a character sketch of Lady Macbeth by reading carefully her soliloquys and her conversations with Macbeth. Estimate the degree to which she seems responsible for convincing Macbeth to do the murder.

Reference: I, 5 (her <u>two</u> soliloquys)

I, 6 (her "greeting of Duncan")

I, 7 (her argument with Macbeth)

4. (a) In Act One Macbeth weighs the pros and cons of murdering Duncan. up in his soliloquy "If it were done, when 'tis done"

(I, 7) Analyze this speech, explaining:
– Macbeth's fears
– the reasons he gives against the murder
– the one reason he gives for the murder

(b) All through Act One, Macbeth's "conscience" has "spoken" to him through "horrid images". Examine some of these images with a view to explaining the depth of his conscience.

Reference: I, 3 (sol. "Two truths are told")

I, 4 (Macbeth's aside, I 47 ff)

I, 7 ("If it we-re done etc.")

Act Two

5. (a) Despite his decision to carry out the murder of Duncan, Macbeth has not fully steeled himself to the crime. Examine and discuss his feelings just before the murder and immediately after. Pay close attention to the imagery of "sleep", "blood" and "darkness".

Reference: II, 1 ("dagger" soliloquy)

II, 2

(b) Compare the reactions of Macduff, Banquo, Lady Macbeth and Macbeth himself to the "news" of Duncan's Murder, and estimate the extent to which the murder plan has been successful.

Act Three

6. Compare the Macbeth that "Scotland" sees with the one we see in Act III, where he is now king and now plotting new murders.

Reference: III, 1, 11. 10-45

Macbeth's sol. "To be thus is nothing"

(a close examination of this.)

III, 2 (look at the imagery here)

7. To what extent is the banquet scene (III, 4) the turning point in Macbeth's life (personally, politically, and ethically). Consider the reasons for the "ghost's" appearance, Macbeth's reaction to it, and the philosophy he announces at the end of the scene. Estimate the damage done to his marriage, to his own "soul".

Reference: III, 4

8. (a) Discuss the reasons for Macbeth's returning to the witches, and his reactions to their "prophecies".

    b) How can you account for his dual attitude towards them? (he "believes" them, yet "curses" them).

    c) Discuss the extent of their "powers" and why, for Shakespeare, they were good dramatic symbols for evil.

Reference: IV, 1.

9. (a) Compare the three "murders" committed by Macbeth (Duncan, Banguo, Lady Macduff and her children) under the following headings.

    1. Macbeth's motives

    2. the manner in which the murder was planned.

    3. the way in which it was carried out

    4. Macbeth's feelings before and after the event.

    (b) How do these murders clearly mark the deterioration in Macbeth's character?

Reference: I, 7 (Sol. "If it were done")

    II, 1 and 2.

    III, 1, 11. 48 -141. III, 3, 4 (reaction to Banquo's ghost)

    IV, 1, 11. 145 -end

    V, 2

Act Five

10. Discuss the "Nemesis" that overtakes Lady Macbeth, commenting on the reasons for her "madness", her nightmares, her need for light, her obsession with blood. To what extent is she a pathetic figure?

Reference: V, 1

    (Re-read her opening soliloquys, (I, 5) and also her reactions to the murder of Duncan (II, 2).

11. In the last act, Macbeth is again seen from the outside (by the Scottish and English Lords, by the Doctor, by Macduff and Malcolm) and from the inside. (We see and hear him as they cannot).

Show that, from the outside, Macbeth appears as "a bloody tyrant"; but that, from the inside, our vantage-point, he appears in a different light: a deranged, old man with flashes of former greatness. Considering both views, to what extent do you find him pitiable? repulsive?

Phase IV Follow-Up: Doing and Viewing

The class has now 'been through' the play three times: they have listened to the 'whole' and heard its constituent 'parts'; they have read and listened; they have re-read; and, at all stages, have talked out their responses. Some kind of consensus has been reached, a first synthesis achieved. A new kind of confidence has been built—through the ear, from the tongue. Old doubts about the eye on the page are beginning to dissipate. It is a time for doing—for going to see a live production, or putting a scene or two on stage, perhaps even reading another tragedy. It is also a time to view a film of the play, to see a new 'reading' of it, now that their own reading has been accomplished. They may even be ready to compare several film versions, more certain now that the old irresistible pull of visual literality can not only be resisted but fully integrated into a new synthesis which includes the vital rhythms of drama (heard and experienced), the *gestalt* power of its poetic language (heard and felt), and the full splendor of its spectacle (seen and now, at last, understood).

Some Principles of Question-Design

English Journal Vol. 70, #7

One challenge we face as literature teachers is that of providing students with questions on a major work which will allow them to explore it with some independence. For example, we often need a large, overview question near the end of the study of a novel to serve as a summative test or as a way of having students, in discussion groups, create their own synthesis. Or we wish students, in groups or independently, to explore a complementary novel free from our intervention.

In either case, if we do not provide enough structure in our questions, students may not be able to sustain an analysis on their own, or they may lose the desired focus, or simply lose heart. On the other hand, if the question is too detailed or composed of too many minor tasks, the teacher might as well teach the material more directly, for the teacher's presence will be felt in the overstructured question, and the students' independence will be curtailed. For example, the teacher who assigns, for an essay or group discussion, simple topics like "The Role of Farfrae in *The Mayor of Casterbridge*" or "The Western Hero in *Shane*" is likely to find only a few advanced students able to write successful essays or provide leadership in a discussion. Many students are dazed by such open-ended tasks; others take the opportunity to waffle or give opinions at great length with little reference to the text or concern for careful re-reading and synthesis. Equally diverse results are likely when students are given a dozen small questions to guide their interpretation of theme or character analysis. Advanced readers feel constrained; others, though more comfortable, are not challenged to make genuine interpretive leaps. Students need the opportunity to hazard predictions, to commit themselves to a personal response, and to feel not too discomfited by the vulnerability of being on their own.

The issue involved in achieving these latter, worthwhile goals is essentially a pedagogical one. We need to know how to compose significant questions—ones which compel re-reading and textual constraints and at the same time encourage independent interpretation, response, and hypothesizing. We need to know how the structuring of major questions affects the way students behave. How do questions direct them as they think and/or talk their way through the constituent tasks *vis-à-vis* the text and their own situations (member of a discussion group, independent readers, alone, *etc.*)? What follows is a set of general principles for constructing such questions, with examples to illustrate their application.

The Principles

Major questions should be composed of some or all of these parts:

The Frame: one or more statements/questions that define the topic. A good frame should *focus* on the subject to be explored–a theme, a central conflict, a major device and its effect–and suggest the *range* of analysis and the particular *Angles* from which it will be approached.

The Task: one or more statements/questions outlining clearly what specific tasks students will do to complete the analysis implied in the Frame. Verb phrases such as *illustrate, give examples, list images, comment upon,* and *compare* are used to direct and limit analysis or discussion. The task-statement may also add more specific angles to the general ones supplied by the Frame.

Angles: these may appear in the Frame and/or the Task. They provide students with clear perspectives on the question as it relates to the text, *e.g.,* "The hero is *brave, resourceful and humane*; illustrate with reference to . . ." or "Looking at the heroine's relationship with her mother and her feelings for her father, comment upon. . . ."

Textual Cues: these may appear in the Frame but are more common in the Task where they serve to direct students to specific parts of the text to help them complete the question raised. They are usually references to specific actions, episodes, conversations, or descriptive passages. They may also be references to specific pages or chapters in the text.

The Question Sequence: following the analysis implied by the Frame and elaborated in the Task, the teacher may add a series of short, probing questions which build upon insights gained from the former detailed study. These are usually experiential, calling on students to bring their own feelings and knowledge to bear on the subject. When used in a series, these questions should be progressively more demanding in their level of inference and should move progressively from the literal text to the experience of the text to the students' own judgments about that experience.

As the examples will show, many constituent elements–Frame, Task, Angles, Cues, Question Sequence–may be rearranged and combined in a variety of ways. In more inductive questions, Tasks, Angles, and Cues may be spread throughout a sequence of shorter questions whose sum total may merely imply the Frame (focus and scope) of the exercise. In some deductive questions, the Frame may be a quotation or interpretive statement against which the Task resonates. Some Frames themselves may suggest specific Angles and Cues, leaving only a single task-word necessary; such as, "Comment on the validity of this statement," or "Discuss the extent to which this statement is true."

The inclusion of phrases such as "to what extent," "to what degree," "which character (event, image) is *more (most)* involved," "which position is *closer* to your own?" are necessary to avoid yes/no responses and to compel real analysis (careful re-reading) and thoughtful discussion.

The content and interpretive implications of large questions will, of course, be dictated by the nature of the text itself. Though each text is unique, the teacher may look for key episodes or patterns of episodes, significant statements by author or characters, and major configurations of character-interaction (father against son, hero versus villain) from which to derive the themes and moral questions that go to making up the Frame and its major Angles. There should be a nice fit between the whole question and parts of the text that inspired it. In deductive questions, the students *reverse* the process gone through by the teacher, beginning with the Frame, exploring the episodes through the Angles provided, and finishing, ideally, with an interpretation structured by the question but not confined to it so long as the final sequence opens the text to their own experience and judgment. In inductive questions, students follow the *same* process gone through by the teacher, beginning with episodes and following a carefully sequenced series of questions which include Tasks, Angles, and Cues and in sum create a Frame. These too should shape an interpretation but leave room at the end for independent judgment.

Examples of Major Questions

Overview question on *Shane* by Jack Schaefer: Deductive Type. In chapters 12 and 13 the qualities of love, loyalty, friendship, and moral and physical courage are displayed as the story reaches its most intense crisis. Give examples to illustrate each of the above. Why is Shane's decision the most difficult of his entire life? (Review past events in the story in preparing your answer.)

The Frame: the first sentence is the Frame, providing a focus (certain "qualities" during an "intense crisis"), Angles ("love," "loyalty," "friendship," "moral and physical courage"), and a Textual Cue (chapters 12 and 13).

The Task: "Give examples to illustrate each." A further Task is added in "Review past events."

The Question Sequence: only one is given here in "Why is Shane's decision the most difficult of his entire life?" However, "most difficult" calls for personal judgment, moral discussion, and a great deal of high-level inference regarding past "decision(s)."

This question is mainly deductive–illustrating given traits–until the final task, where it becomes more open-ended.

Overview question on a single theme in *True Grit* by Charles Portis: Inductive Type. Mattie Ross hires Rooster Cogburn not because he is her ideal heroic man but because he is said to have "true grit." (a) What aspects of Rooster's personality and behavior would make him less than a hero in our eyes? Consider his past activities, his behavior as a marshal, his habits, his motives, and general outlook on life. (b) What things about Rooster does Mattie particularly dislike at first? Consider here Mattie's own character, prejudices, *etc.* (c) At the end of the story, Mattie has come to respect Rooster (perhaps even love him). Why has she changed her mind? What admirable qualities (that Maggie might have missed) does Rooster show us, the readers, from his first appearance in the book? (d) To what extent is LaBoeuf an admirable character? Did you expect him to behave as he did at the end of the story? Did Mattie? Explain.

The Frame: this is largely an inductive question on the various implications of the theme of the hero. Hence, the Frame is brief (the first sentence), setting the focus and general Angles   ("ideal heroic man" versus "true grit").

The Question Sequence: parts *a* to *d* explore, inductively, the hero-theme. They demand a high degree of inference and are textually quite open. The Tasks are spread throughout ("What aspects," "Consider," "What things," "Why has she . . . ?" and "What qualities . . . ?" etc.) and integrated with the Angles ("personality and behavior," "past activities," "at first," "the end of the story," "his first appearance"). Part *c* contains a small Frame of its own ("Mattie has come to respect Rooster"). The result, then, of this series of inductive questions is a free-wheeling, textually open exploration of the hero-theme with a fair degree of inference demanded *en route*. Note, again, the use of *"What* aspects," *"What* things," and "To what extent" to ensure that students must select among items, weigh them, and come to some judgment.

This question would be ideal for group discussion because it balances textual constraints and the demands for student interpretation.

Major question on form for advanced readers from *True Grit*. This is a "frame novel" where the narrator, Mattie Ross, tells the story as an old woman looking back to her fourteenth year. What evidence throughout the story do we have of this technique? Give at least five examples of comments or events that relate to a time beyond the main story. How do these examples help to give us a sharper sense of Mattie the girl and Mattie the woman, their similarities and differences? What would the story lose if it were told directly from the view of the fourteen-year-old Mattie?

The Frame: the first sentence is the Frame, focusing on the technique ("frame novel") and explaining generally how it operates in the novel. Since some prior knowledge and experience with the technique are called for, this question is for advanced readers.

The Task: students are asked initially to find "five examples" of the technique with no Cues provided. Then they must show how the technique works to develop the two sides of Mattie's character, using the Angles provided ("the girl," "the woman," "similarities," "differences").

The Question Sequence: the last sentence of the assignment provides a very open and demanding question in which students are asked to assess the effects of the technique by re-imagining the story from a single rather than a double viewpoint. Individual judgment and interpretation are called for.

This question would be suitable for a group of advanced readers. They might be given some time to discuss it as a group, then asked to write out their independent response in essay form.

Varying the Degree of Difficulty

Once the use of the basic elements of question construction has been mastered, the teacher may then manipulate these to create a variety of inductive and deductive tasks and to vary the level of difficulty for specific grades, classes, groups, or individual students. For example, the following question on *Boss of the Namko Drive* by Paul St. Pierre is relatively easy, having been designed for less able readers at the grade nine level.

Delore learns a great deal by watching and interacting with the adults around him. For each of the following characters, discuss what Delore learns, how he learns (observation, talk, action), and how much his view of the adult world changes as a result: Step-and-a-Half; Walter Charlie; Frenchie (at the beginning); Anatole Harry; Mathoose; and Frenchie (at the end). Give specific examples to prove your point.

The level of difficulty could be increased by:

Removing the Angles from the complex *show how* Task ("observation, talk, action)" and replacing them with a general Angle ("three ways").

Removing the Cues ("Step-and-a-half," "Walter Charlie," *etc.*) and replacing them with a Task demanding selection and discrimination, e.g., "Selecting the three most important adults, discuss what Delore learns . . . "

Collapsing the three carefully sequenced Tasks ("discuss what . . . how . . . how much") into a single, more abstract Task, *e.g.,* "Discuss Delore's gradual development from boyhood to manhood as a result of his interaction with three of the adults."

The level of difficulty could be further decreased by:

Adding specific textual Cues to the character Cues, *i.e.,* page references or references to key episodes involving the character and Delore (with or without page references), omitting the second, more demanding *show how* Task altogether, leaving only "discuss what Delore learns and how much his view of . . . "

Replacing "discuss" with "tell."

Replacing "for each of" with "for any two of."

Here are some general principles for varying the level of difficultly of large questions.

Deductive questions are generally easier than inductive ones provided that the Frame is free of abstract language and technical terminology, that Tasks are of the *give examples* type, and that adequate Cues are provided.

Inductive questions, though generally harder because less is given and more demanded, can be simplified by careful sequencing (content–specific interpretation of an episode–more general/experiential inference) and by providing adequate Cues.

General Angles are more difficult to handle than specific ones.

Detailed Tasks, broken into steps with simple task-words are easier than single-statement Tasks like "discuss" or "comment."

In general, it will be the overall degree of *structuring* which will determine the relative difficulty of the assignment – light structuring is most demanding, heavy structuring the least demanding, with many gradations between. Both inductive and deductive questions can be constructed so that they are lightly, moderately, or heavily structured.

Here are examples of inductive questions at three levels, for *Jamie* by Jack Bennett: (a) Discuss the various ways in which Jamie matures during the course of the novel (light structuring). (b) Discuss at least three ways in which Jamie matures during the course of the novel. Refer to specific changes in character traits as he moves from boy to man (moderate structuring). (c) Point out three boy-like character traits revealed by Jamie in chapters 1-14. Show how these traits develop into mature adult ones by referring to three major events in chapters 15-32 (heavy structuring).

Here are examples of deductive questions at three levels: (a) Jamie changes from a playful, carefree boy to a courageous, responsible adult. Illustrate with reference to the novel (light). (b) Jamie changes from an innocent, carefree, loving boy to a mature, morally responsible, courageous adult with a somewhat embittered view of experience. Illustrate with reference to four major episodes (moderate). (c) Jamie changes from an innocent, carefree loving boy to a mature, morally responsible, courageous adult with a somewhat embittered view of experience. Illustrate with reference to his reactions to his father's death, his attempts to cope with the drought, his rescue of the drowning cow, and his encounter with the buffalo (heavy).

In the case of both inductive and deductive questions, it is important to note that light structuring is significantly more demanding than moderate or heavy structuring. Only advanced readers who already know how to analyze a novel and who have a genuine interest in it will be able to sustain a group discussion on a lightly structured question. Average readers will need teacher intervention to keep them going. Weak readers will flounder before they begin if Angles and Cues, which provide extra structure, are not given.

Therefore, the teacher who wishes students to work in groups or individually must be certain that the type of question–inductive or deductive–and its level of structuring are appropriate to the group or student involved. Moderate to heavy structuring is advisable for all but very advanced and independent students. However, as the preceding section demonstrates, levels of difficulty can be shifted substantially within even a heavily structured question by manipulating the language of Frames, Angles, and Tasks; by adjusting the specificity of Cues; and by adding challenging inferential sequences to the final part of any major question.

Conclusion

As Frank Smith noted in *Understanding Reading,* a teacher's questions are much more than pedagogical gimmickry or a matter of instructional "style." They are an intrinsic part of the complex and little understood process of reading itself. Our understanding of our own questions and their behavioral and cognitive consequences is still in its infancy, but it is a goal worth pursuing because the stakes are high.

– 04 –

Some Principles of Question-Design

English Journal Vol. 70, #7

One challenge we face as literature teachers is that of providing students with questions on a major work which will allow them to explore it with some independence. For example, we often need a large, overview question near the end of the study of a novel to serve as a summative test or as a way of having students, in discussion groups, create their own synthesis. Or we wish students, in groups or independently, to explore a complementary novel free from our intervention.

In either case, if we do not provide enough structure in our questions, students may not be able to sustain an analysis on their own, or they may lose the desired focus, or simply lose heart. On the other hand, if the question is too detailed or composed of too many minor tasks, the teacher might as well teach the material more directly, for the teacher's presence will be felt in the overstructured question, and the students' independence will be curtailed. For example, the teacher who assigns, for an essay or group discussion, simple topics like "The Role of Farfrae in *The Mayor of Casterbridge*" or "The Western Hero in *Shane*" is likely to find only a few advanced students able to write successful essays or provide leadership in a discussion. Many students are dazed by such open-ended tasks; others take the opportunity to waffle or give opinions at great length with little reference to the text or concern for careful re-reading and synthesis. Equally diverse results are likely when students are given a dozen small questions to guide their interpretation of theme or character analysis. Advanced readers feel constrained; others, though more comfortable, are not challenged to make genuine interpretive leaps. Students need the opportunity to hazard predictions, to commit themselves to a personal response, and to feel not too discomfited by the vulnerability of being on their own.

The issue involved in achieving these latter, worthwhile goals is essentially a pedagogical one. We need to know how to compose significant questions—ones which compel re-reading and textual constraints and at the same time encourage independent interpretation, response, and hypothesizing. We need to know how the structuring of major questions affects the way students behave. How do questions direct them as they think and/or talk their way through the constituent tasks *vis-à-vis* the text and their own situations (member of a discussion group, independent readers, alone, *etc.*)? What follows is a set of general principles for constructing such questions, with examples to illustrate their application.

The Principles

Major questions should be composed of some or all of these parts:

The Frame: one or more statements/questions that define the topic. A good frame should *focus* on the subject to be explored–a theme, a central conflict, a major device and its effect–and suggest the *range* of analysis and the particular *Angles* from which it will be approached.

The Task: one or more statements/questions outlining clearly what specific tasks students will do to complete the analysis implied in the Frame. Verb phrases such as *illustrate, give examples, list images, comment upon,* and *compare* are used to direct and limit analysis or discussion. The task-statement may also add more specific angles to the general ones supplied by the Frame.

Angles: these may appear in the Frame and/or the Task. They provide students with clear perspectives on the question as it relates to the text, *e.g.,* "The hero is *brave, resourceful and humane*; illustrate with reference to . . ." or "Looking at the heroine's relationship with her mother and her feelings for her father, comment upon. . . ."

Textual Cues: these may appear in the Frame but are more common in the Task where they serve to direct students to specific parts of the text to help them complete the question raised. They are usually references to specific actions, episodes, conversations, or descriptive passages. They may also be references to specific pages or chapters in the text.

The Question Sequence: following the analysis implied by the Frame and elaborated in the Task, the teacher may add a series of short, probing questions which build upon insights gained from the former detailed study. These are usually experiential, calling on students to bring their own feelings and knowledge to bear on the subject. When used in a series, these questions should be progressively more demanding in their level of inference and should move progressively from the literal text to the experience of the text to the students' own judgments about that experience.

As the examples will show, many constituent elements–Frame, Task, Angles, Cues, Question Sequence–may be rearranged and combined in a variety of ways. In more inductive questions, Tasks, Angles, and Cues may be spread throughout a sequence of shorter questions whose sum total may merely imply the Frame (focus and scope) of the exercise. In some deductive questions, the Frame may be a quotation or interpretive statement against which the Task resonates. Some Frames themselves may suggest specific Angles and Cues, leaving only a single task-word necessary; such as, "Comment on the validity of this statement," or "Discuss the extent to which this statement is true."

The inclusion of phrases such as "to what extent," "to what degree," "which character (event, image) is *more (most)* involved," "which position is *closer* to your own?"

are necessary to avoid yes/no responses and to compel real analysis (careful re-reading) and thoughtful discussion.

The content and interpretive implications of large questions will, of course, be dictated by the nature of the text itself. Though each text is unique, the teacher may look for key episodes or patterns of episodes, significant statements by author or characters, and major configurations of character-interaction (father against son, hero versus villain) from which to derive the themes and moral questions that go to making up the Frame and its major Angles. There should be a nice fit between the whole question and parts of the text that inspired it. In deductive questions, the students *reverse* the process gone through by the teacher, beginning with the Frame, exploring the episodes through the Angles provided, and finishing, ideally, with an interpretation structured by the question but not confined to it so long as the final sequence opens the text to their own experience and judgment. In inductive questions, students follow the *same* process gone through by the teacher, beginning with episodes and following a carefully sequenced series of questions which include Tasks, Angles, and Cues and in sum create a Frame. These too should shape an interpretation but leave room at the end for independent judgment.

Examples of Major Questions

Overview question on *Shane* by Jack Schaefer: Deductive Type. In chapters 12 and 13 the qualities of love, loyalty, friendship, and moral and physical courage are displayed as the story reaches its most intense crisis. Give examples to illustrate each of the above. Why is Shane's decision the most difficult of his entire life? (Review past events in the story in preparing your answer.)

The Frame: the first sentence is the Frame, providing a focus (certain "qualities" during an "intense crisis"), Angles ("love," "loyalty," "friendship," "moral and physical courage"), and a Textual Cue (chapters 12 and 13).

The Task: "Give examples to illustrate each." A further Task is added in "Review past events."

The Question Sequence: only one is given here in "Why is Shane's decision the most difficult of his entire life?" However, "most difficult" calls for personal judgment, moral discussion, and a great deal of high-level inference regarding past "decision(s)."

This question is mainly deductive–illustrating given traits–until the final task, where it becomes more open-ended.

Overview question on a single theme in *True Grit* by Charles Portis: Inductive Type. Mattie Ross hires Rooster Cogburn not because he is her ideal heroic man but because he is said to have "true grit." (a) What aspects of Rooster's personality and behavior would make him less than a hero in our eyes? Consider his past activities, his behavior as a marshal, his habits, his motives, and general outlook on life. (b) What things about Rooster does Mattie particularly dislike at first? Consider here Mattie's own character, prejudices, *etc.* (c) At the end of the story, Mattie has come to respect Rooster (perhaps even love him). Why has she changed her mind? What admirable qualities (that Maggie might have missed) does Rooster show us, the readers, from his first appearance in the book? (d) To what extent is LaBoeuf an admirable character? Did you expect him to behave as he did at the end of the story? Did Mattie? Explain.

The Frame: this is largely an inductive question on the various implications of the theme of the hero. Hence, the Frame is brief (the first sentence), setting the focus and general Angles   ("ideal heroic man" versus "true grit").

The Question Sequence: parts *a* to *d* explore, inductively, the hero-theme. They demand a high degree of inference and are textually quite open. The Tasks are spread throughout ("What aspects," "Consider," "What things," "Why has she . . . ?" and "What qualities . . . ?" etc.) and integrated with the Angles ("personality and behavior," "past activities," "at first," "the end of the story," "his first appearance"). Part *c* contains a small Frame of its own ("Mattie has come to respect Rooster"). The result, then, of this series of inductive questions is a free-wheeling, textually open exploration of the hero-theme with a fair degree of inference demanded *en route*. Note, again, the use of *"What* aspects," *"What* things," and "To what extent" to ensure that students must select among items, weigh them, and come to some judgment.

This question would be ideal for group discussion because it balances textual constraints and the demands for student interpretation.

Major question on form for advanced readers from *True Grit*. This is a "frame novel" where the narrator, Mattie Ross, tells the story as an old woman looking back to her fourteenth year. What evidence throughout the story do we have of this technique? Give at least five examples of comments or events that relate to a time beyond the main story. How do these examples help to give us a sharper sense of Mattie the girl and Mattie the woman, their similarities and differences? What would the story lose if it were told directly from the view of the fourteen-year-old Mattie?

The Frame: the first sentence is the Frame, focusing on the technique ("frame novel") and explaining generally how it operates in the novel. Since some prior knowledge and experience with the technique are called for, this question is for advanced readers.

The Task: students are asked initially to find "five examples" of the technique with no Cues provided. Then they must show how the technique works to develop the two sides of Mattie's character, using the Angles provided ("the girl," "the woman," "similarities," "differences").

The Question Sequence: the last sentence of the assignment provides a very open and demanding question in which students are asked to assess the effects of the technique by re-imagining the story from a single rather than a double viewpoint. Individual judgment and interpretation are called for.

This question would be suitable for a group of advanced readers. They might be given some time to discuss it as a group, then asked to write out their independent response in essay form.

Varying the Degree of Difficulty

Once the use of the basic elements of question construction has been mastered, the teacher may then manipulate these to create a variety of inductive and deductive tasks and to vary the level of difficulty for specific grades, classes, groups, or individual students. For example, the following question on *Boss of the Namko Drive* by Paul St. Pierre is relatively easy, having been designed for less able readers at the grade nine level.

Delore learns a great deal by watching and interacting with the adults around him. For each of the following characters, discuss what Delore learns, how he learns (observation, talk, action), and how much his view of the adult world changes as a result: Step-and-a-Half; Walter Charlie; Frenchie (at the beginning); Anatole Harry; Mathoose; and Frenchie (at the end). Give specific examples to prove your point.

The level of difficulty could be *increased* by:

Removing the Angles from the complex *show how* Task ("observation, talk, action)" and replacing them with a general Angle ("three ways").

Removing the Cues ("Step-and-a-half," "Walter Charlie," *etc.*) and replacing them with a Task demanding selection and discrimination, e.g., "Selecting the three most important adults, discuss what Delore learns . . . "

Collapsing the three carefully sequenced Tasks ("discuss what . . . how . . . how much") into a single, more abstract Task, *e.g.,* "Discuss Delore's gradual development from boyhood to manhood as a result of his interaction with three of the adults."

The level of difficulty could be further decreased by:

Adding specific textual Cues to the character Cues, *i.e.,* page references or references to key episodes involving the character and Delore (with or without page references), omitting the second, more demanding *show how* Task altogether, leaving only "discuss what Delore learns and how much his view of . . . "

Replacing "discuss" with "tell."

Replacing "for each of" with "for any two of."

Here are some general principles for varying the level of difficultly of large questions.

Deductive questions are generally easier than inductive ones provided that the Frame is free of abstract language and technical terminology, that Tasks are of the *give examples* type, and that adequate Cues are provided.

Inductive questions, though generally harder because less is given and more demanded, can be simplified by careful sequencing (content–specific interpretation of an episode–more general/experiential inference) and by providing adequate Cues.

General Angles are more difficult to handle than specific ones.

Detailed Tasks, broken into steps with simple task-words are easier than single-statement Tasks like "discuss" or "comment."

In general, it will be the overall degree of *structuring* which will determine the relative difficulty of the assignment – light structuring is most demanding, heavy structuring the least demanding, with many gradations between. Both inductive and deductive questions can be constructed so that they are lightly, moderately, or heavily structured.

Here are examples of inductive questions at three levels, for *Jamie* by Jack Bennett: (a) Discuss the various ways in which Jamie matures during the course of the novel (light structuring). (b) Discuss at least three ways in which Jamie matures during the course of the novel. Refer to specific changes in character traits as he moves from boy to man (moderate structuring). (c) Point out three boy-like character traits revealed by Jamie in chapters 1-14. Show how these traits develop into mature adult ones by referring to three major events in chapters 15-32 (heavy structuring).

Here are examples of deductive questions at three levels: (a) Jamie changes from a playful, carefree boy to a courageous, responsible adult. Illustrate with reference to the novel (light). (b) Jamie changes from an innocent, carefree, loving boy to a mature, morally responsible, courageous adult with a somewhat embittered view of experience. Illustrate with reference to four major episodes (moderate). (c) Jamie changes from an innocent, carefree loving boy to a mature, morally responsible, courageous adult with a somewhat embittered view of experience. Illustrate with reference to his reactions to his father's death, his attempts to cope with the drought, his rescue of the drowning cow, and his encounter with the buffalo (heavy).

In the case of both inductive and deductive questions, it is important to note that light structuring is significantly more demanding than moderate or heavy structuring. Only advanced readers who already know how to analyze a novel and who have a genuine interest in it will be able to sustain a group discussion on a lightly structured question. Average readers will need teacher intervention to keep them going. Weak readers will flounder before they begin if Angles and Cues, which provide extra structure, are not given.

Therefore, the teacher who wishes students to work in groups or individually must be certain that the type of question–inductive or deductive–and its level of structuring are appropriate to the group or student involved. Moderate to heavy structuring is advisable for all but very advanced and independent students. However, as the preceding section demonstrates, levels of difficulty can be shifted substantially within even a heavily structured question by manipulating the language of Frames, Angles, and Tasks; by adjusting the specificity of Cues; and by adding challenging inferential sequences to the final part of any major question.

Conclusion

As Frank Smith noted in *Understanding Reading,* a teacher's questions are much more than pedagogical gimmickry or a matter of instructional "style." They are an intrinsic part of the complex and little understood process of reading itself. Our understanding of our own questions and their behavioral and cognitive consequences is still in its infancy, but it is a goal worth pursuing because the stakes are high.

− 05 −

Setting Goals for English:
A Model and Several Cautions

More than enough ink and not a little blood has been spilled during these past three years in the fight for, or against, behavioural objectives in English. Summerfield, Moffett, Hogan, Guth and a host of lesser cohorts have carried the flag (if not the day) with courage and eloquence. We have 'chosen up sides', drawn clear battle lines, and waved our pens mightily for the cause. Little more can or need be said.

What I propose to do is to outline a specific model for writing out our goals (*our* word, not *theirs*) on our terms and for our purposes. That the model may, *en passent*, satisfy the demands for accountability and the clarifying of our goals and procedures is a happy coincidence (or, conversely, 'quite predicable', says the English teacher, who has known all along). At any rate, it will be our *own* model–to use or abuse.

The best way to begin talking with any English teacher is to start with something he is teaching. I bow to that eminently reasonable demand. Simply stated, we are given a short story to teach and asked to explain how and why we are teaching it. The story is "Luke Baldwin's Vow" by Morley Callaghan, selected for our grade eleven programme, to be taught to both the general students (non-academic, slow readers—supply your own euphemism) and the academic ones. For the sake of convenience, I shall use, loosely interpreted, the four levels of objectives suggested by J. N. Hook[1] in his essay in *On Writing Behavioral Objectives for English*. With this task and this framework in mind, we shall work our way down from the motherhood goals to the actual classroom experience, with some tangential remarks along the way.

Level 1: Educational

(1) to have students respond to and share in the vicarious experiences of other people, places, situations with a view to developing a broad understanding of the 'world'

(2) to have students, as a result of (1), develop attitudes of empathy with the experience of others, of tolerance for other points of view, *etc.*

(3) to have students learn more about themselves by confronting new experience with both a critical and an empathetic eye, *etc. etc. etc.*

Level 2: Language/Literature (English)

(1) to have students—through the vicarious experience offered by stories, poems, plays, novels, *etc.*—'suspend their disbelief' long enough to feel, understand and respond critically to *other experience.*

(2) to have students process the other experience of literature so that it broadens their view of man, the world, *etc.*; makes them examine their own responses to experience; and promotes among them a tolerance for other views through a willingness to hold "hateful contraries" simultaneously in the mind (ambiguities, ambivalences, open-ended 'questions', *etc.*)

(3) to have students—through their reading and writing, listening and talking—come to see that language through its 'literary' manifestations processes experience in a way which objectifies it for contemplation, study, and response, and makes (1) and (2) possible.

(4) to have students develop the skill areas—reading, writing, listening, talking—*operationally* and in the *context* of the experiences outlined above (*i.e.* skill *in* language operations and knowledge *through* language experience)

(5) to have students, through an assiduous application of the foregoing goals, 'use' language/literature to understand their own experience (psychological and sociological) in ways which they come to find meaningful; this *cannot* and *should not* be specified further, for in the final analysis the uses of literacy and literature are open questions; we can only describe some of the innumerable affects, (*e.g.*, as above, as well as other spin-offs like clarity of 'thinking', a whole corncrib full of communi-cations 'skills', the moral implications of literary training (see William Walsh, *The Use of Imagination*), *etc.* But as Frye says in *The Well-Tempered Critic*, it is ultimately a question of *belief*; language and its rhetorics are a fundamental symbol-system, and literature in some form has been a part of every civilization. Is this not enough?) We can list affects interminably; and we should be aware of them; but we cannot predict them with any accuracy. They are at best 'may-do' behaviours.

(6a) to have students, in the *academic programme*, achieve the foregoing by coming to process literary materials (receptive and expressive phases) rhetorically, *i.e.* they should be aware of the form—content synthesis; they should be able to progressively articulate their responses to the meaning—structure complex in literature—their own as well as others—and always in an operational context.

b) to have students, in the *general programme*, achieve the foregoing by coming to process literary materials (receptive and expressive phases) in close context with their "real-life" experience; rhetorical skills needed to respond to the materials should be handled indirectly and only as required—the students' successful processing of the literature should be accepted as evidence of their rhetorical skill (implied rather than articulated).

Level 3: Instructional/e.g. The Short Story "Luke Baldwin's Vow"

A – Academic Approach

Rhetorical Goals   Experiential Goals

to have students come to understand the character of Uncle Henry and Luke looking at the methods Callaghan uses to present them (descriptive detail, author comment, dialogue, interaction of characters, point of view)   through a response to plot and character development, to have students see and feel the conflict between a practical man and an imaginative, affectionate boy

to have students see that Uncle Henry and Luke represent conflicting attitudes toward life (practical versus imaginative, *etc.*); *i.e.* they are 'symbolic' in a general sense to have students feel the direction and nature of the authors sympathies (with Luke) by responding to plot, point of view, *etc.*

to have students see that this is a story of character giving rise to themes or statements about experience, and that this is made clear (1) in the introductory paragraphs, (2) in the plot development which merely intensifies the basic conflicts, (3) in the final paragraph – Luke's summary statement, (4) in the title   to   have students discuss the questions raised about these two attitudes towards experience, with a view to making up their own minds (do they agree with Callaghan's viewpoint? Is there any sympathy here for Uncle Henry?, *etc.*

to have students, individually, and in groups, read other Callaghan stories, using any rhetorical understanding gained from this story   to have students take the story into their own experience: is the conflict here still an important one in our society? *etc.*

to have students read other Callaghan stories looking at the moral questions raised and explored

B – General Approach

Experiential Goals

– to have students see and feel the conflict between Uncle Henry and Luke (1) by looking at them as individuals (with structured questions from the teacher to guide them through Callaghan's methods of characterization), (2) by looking at the conflict raised by the dog and its effects on Luke and Uncle Henry, (3) by tracing the plot development through, with a view to seeing how it complicates the character conflict and is 'resolved'

— to have students feel the author's sympathies (mainly through the plot or 'action', and the natural sympathy given to an orphan boy and a poor old half-blind dog, *etc.*)

— to have students discuss the questions raised by the story with a view to exploring their own sympathies and attitudes as well as the author's

— to have students discuss the relevance of the story's moral implications for their own society (the practical versus the sentimental, *etc.*)

— to have students to go on to read other Callaghan stories (with structured questions initially to guide them through the rhetorical difficulties)

Rhetorical Goals

— these are limited and implied only: 17 year olds have a firm conception of *plot* at its simplest level; some help is needed to get them through *characterization* and direct them to the thematic implications of the story

— we expect only minor *specific transfer* from one story to the next; what transfer or rhetorical reading skill which does occur will be learned *implicitly* from the *whole* story and the cumulative nature of the discussion.

Level 4 The Lesson/Questions and Sequence

For details, see Appendix

In order to prepare proper pedagogical questions and a sequence of lessons, the teacher works primarily from such goals as stated above at Level 3. Those goals can be seen as being related vertically to some or all of the general goals for English (Level 2) and for the educational system (Level 1).

In brief, the questions and sequencing of activities 'contain' the goals for the unit, the course, and the school. Beginning teachers would do well to write out goals at Level 3 for at least some individual works and most of their units. Experienced teachers, however, learn to eliminate or drastically reduce the writing out of goals at Level 3 by becoming skilled at formulating questions and lesson sequences which imply specific goals at all levels. Level 3 goals in particular are subsumed by the intelligent formulation of complex, 'large' questions in which rhetorical and experiential responses are *necessary* concomitants to exploring and 'solving' them.

Level 4 goals (especially of a behavioural variety) are of minimal value, even for the beginning teacher; for example, in this unit, such objectives might include the defining of the constituent elements of the plot, the specific parts of each of the five methods of characterization (with numerous examples from the text), the enumeration of a dozen or more specific ways in which students *might* state the theme, *etc.* Such formulations are made by the teacher as he reads the text in the light of his other goals (Levels 1-3), and as he prepares questions which will direct students into the text. His own response will be complex and multi-dimensional (*e.g.,* plot, character, emotional structuring and response) and the questions themselves should result from his 'reading' and be designed to take students through the text toward their own responses to it. Of course, the teacher must learn to expect and anticipate specific student responses. On the other hand, to state or write out *all* expected responses in detailed behaviouralist terms is to limit students in a way which is contrary to the open-endedness of the literary experience (*e.g.,* what *does* a symbol finally, ultimately, absolutely mean? Where does the connotation of an image really end?). To attempt such a procedure would involve, in the least, writing down thousands of responses, without any guarantee of getting them all. More importantly, there is no way of putting these anticipated 'behaviours' in any reasonable sequence. The students' response, like the teacher's or that of any 'right reader', will be multi-dimensional. At best, we can formulate questions which incorporate goals at Level 3 and beyond, which have some natural sequence, and which provide a number of angles for processing the story (a division of 'parts' is implied here, but kept at a level general enough to allow for multiple responses, designed to keep rhetorical considerations closely allied with affective ones, and flexible enough to be adapted to suit the actual classroom situation).

The experienced teacher learns to predict with some degree of accuracy the kinds and levels of response from individual classes and groupings to particular texts. He does so by framing and reframing questions to meet Level 3 goals, and by monitoring student responses *in situ*. In brief he learns his art by adapting such question and sequences as he observes their *effectiveness* and *affectiveness* in 'real' classroom situations. And it is precisely in this area of our work that much can be achieved in improving instruction. To work the other way—by trying to delineate hundreds or even thousands of anticipated behaviours for which there is no logical or psychological sequence and which do not account for the complexity of response natural to language structures—this direction is counter-productive. To provide assistance and advice for young teachers in formulating appropriate questions and lesson-sequences and to facilitate goal-setting for English courses in a given department or school system—these are the primary concerns of those who wish to improve the standard of instruction and consequent levels of student-learning. And they can be best achieved by having English teachers: (1) discuss their local educational goals in the light of their present courses of study; (2) formulate periodically (every three or four years?) general goals for the English programme, except for new courses where precise objectives should be drawn up before implementation; (3) discuss, at Level 3, the classroom objectives and procedures for major items on each course at each grade or level—these should not necessarily be written out, so long as the questions, tests, assignments and methodologies are scrutinized in the light of higher-level goals; the exception here would be inexperienced teachers who might be asked to select major parts of their courses (sample stories, writing units, media projects, *etc.*) and draw up classroom objectives as well as related procedures, questions, assignments and tests.

Such a review would ensure that significant emphasis was being placed upon goal-setting; it would also ensure that accountability and the evaluation of teachers (and 'learning') was made possible without destroying the program in the process. For example, those in the hierarchy to whom we are accountable—principals, supervisors, *etc.*—should be invited to attend the discussions mentioned above; department heads should also be prepared to discuss Level 3 goals at any time, and to present as required such documents as course descriptions, outlines, and sample units with full apparatus including student work. The task of evaluating the learning at the level of the individual teacher and the classroom, however, should and can be done by the department head, the subject supervisor and senior teachers. This difficult task will be immensely facilitated when the beginning teacher has been exposed to departmental goal-setting discussions before and during his initial teacher year. Furthermore, specific evaluation of the learning being achieved by his students can be accomplished in two basic ways. (1) The formulation of questions and lesson-sequences subsuming goals at Level 3 and beyond should be examined outside of and during the classroom experience. Here, the teacher takes responsibility for formulating such questions and procedures which can be discussed in the abstract and/or in the actual teaching environment. Properly formulated, they should effect responses from the students (in their talk and through their writing) which can be 'measured' against stated goals. It should not be necessary for either teacher or supervisor to predict *specific* behavioural outcomes (Level 4) but merely, in context, to discuss what the students have said/written in view of the earlier goal-setting sessions. With an intelligent 'sampling' of the teacher's/student's work, a fair assessment of the teacher's ability to frame goal-oriented questions and achieve some degree of success can be made without resorting to the laborious, time-wasting, counter-productive procedure of writing down all goals at all levels. After all, we *are* dealing with highly trained professionals who, while they may be inexperienced or undertrained as teachers, do know something about language and literature and the kinds of demands and affects it entails for any human being who uses or confronts it. (2) When teachers need assistance, they can be given help with the formulation of Level 2 goals and appropriate questions and methods after which their effectiveness in carrying these forward into the learning experience can again be 'measured' in the terms outlined in (1) above. This procedure allows for a two-stage evaluation where required; *i.e.* each new teacher, after some induction through the departmental discussions of goal-setting, would be free to set his own questions and sequences, with periodic monitoring and assistance. If the monitoring revealed a need for further guidance, the second stage could be implemented in which the department head and/or senior teachers would assist in developing suitable questions and sequences for the teacher concerned, followed by a detailed evaluation in the classroom context.

Finally: in implementing this evaluation/accountability model care should be taken to keep the amount of written material to the absolute minimum at all levels (1-3); minimal goals may be succinctly defined in written terms, and then followed by the fullest possible consultation, discussion, and self-appraisal. The preparation of curriculum materials at Level 2 and 3 and their subsequent 'evaluation' should be carried out as *examples* of what has to be done and not as all there is to be done. Thus, the individual teacher is given some freedom to exploit his talent and that of his students so that goals at Levels 1, 2, and 3 can be achieved gradually, intermittently, and humanely. Conversely, he can be called to account for his teaching at any time, knowing that a selected sampling of his work is all that is necessary, and that if he does not meet the standards required he will be given advice and support. Ideally, then, self-criticism is still possible in spite of these external controls; personal growth can be encouraged in an atmosphere free of real anxiety; and a sense of collective responsibility promoted within departments of English and a school system seething with the unrest and frustration common to hierarchical structures.

NOTES
1 – J. N. Hook, "The Tri-University BOE Project: a Progress Report", in *On Writing Behavioral*
2 – *Objectives For English*, NCTE, 1970.

APPENDIX:Lesson Plans for "Luke Baldwin's Vow"

TEXT: *A Harvest of Short Stories*, Longmans, Toronto, 1960.

A.ACADEMIC, GRADE 11

Preparation: Read the Story before class.

LESSON ONE

Questions:

1)Where does the introduction end? Why?

What purpose does it serve? – plot

– character

– setting

Which basic element dominates here?

2)How is the character of Uncle Henry made clear to us?

– action

– speech

– author comment

– other points of view

– descriptive detail

3) How is the character of Luke presented? Why is the setting important for an understanding of his character?

4) What conflicts, internal and external, are presented through the characters?

5) In what ways is Dan likely to be the central figure in the plot development (or in the complications of the various conflicts)?

HOMEWORK: the body of the story

1) The story moves toward its resolution through at least three crises.

a) Indicate the crises, and show how the action serves to reinforce, complicate, and emotionally intensify the basic character conflict.

b) What methods does Callaghan use to control our sympathies in this section of the story?

LESSON TWO

Discuss homework questions, focussing on how the essential character conflict is worked out through the "action", and how our response is controlled by Callaghan's carefully selected detail, and by the use of Luke as narrator.

HOMEWORK: the resolution

1.a) In what way does Mr. Kemp's proposal appear to resolve the basic issue of the external conflict?

b) How has Callaghan prepared us for Mr. Kemp's intervention?

2.) The internal conflict in Uncle Henry, hinted at in the introduction, is fully revealed in the last section of the story by the following means:

– the direct confrontation between Luke and Uncle Henry and what each stands for.

– the device whereby the author lets us see, for the first time, into the mind and feelings of Uncle Henry.

– external descriptive detail.

Discuss.

3.a) To what extent have all the conflicts been resolved at the end?

b) Is the resolution satisfying, structurally and emotionally? Explain.

4.) Through the use of a basic contrast of character, the title, and Luke's final comment (the last paragraph), the reader becomes aware that Luke and his Uncle come to represent (or symbolize) two conflicting views of life, and that the ironies involved in the resolution hold a deeper meaning for us about the essential values in life. Discuss, with appropriate references. (to be *written* in essay form)

LESSON THREE

Discuss homework questions. #4 could be left as a suitable follow-up assignment to Lesson Three.

FOLLOW-UP

1.) Other Callaghan stories could be studied with a focus on the way in which the author uses character and action to elucidate basic "themes" and to direct the reader's sympathy so that he becomes newly aware of human dilemmas.

The academic student should be consciously aware that he is transferring *rhetorical* skills to his new reading in order to deepen his personal response to literature as structured experience.

2.) Other stories of character or ones with moral themes could be compared with Callaghan's—thematically, emotively, and rhetorically.

B. *GENERAL, GRADE 11*

– Preparation: students read the story before class.

LESSON ONE. Reread the first eight paragraphs *aloud* in class.

Questions

1.a) What circumstances brought Luke to Uncle Henry's place?

b) What was Uncle Henry like? What did he look like? How did he go about running his mill? How did he "take care of" his dead brother's child? What did his wife think of him? The men around the mill?

c)Discuss Luke's feelings for and opinions about Uncle Henry. In what way were they coloured by the vow he made to his dying father?

2.a) Describe Luke's life at the mill.

b)What activities brought him the most happiness?

c)In what ways was he not perfectly happy? Why?

d) In summary, what sort of boy was Luke?

3.a) What were Uncle Henry's feelings about Dan? Why would you expect this reaction from him?

b) Explain the importance of the dog in Luke's life. How do his feelings for Dan differ from Uncle Henry's?

4.a) What conflict do you see arising as the story progresses? Why might Dan play a central role?

b) What emotional conflict could arise in Luke's mind as a result?

c) Is Uncle Henry perfectly happy? (what are those strange "aches and pains" he has in his back?)

d) Do you know any people like Uncle Henry? Like Luke? What would you feel if you were Luke?

e) Whose "side" is Callaghan on?

HOMEWORK pp. 57-63 (#3 to be written)

1. The exciting incidents (or crises) in this story concern Luke's efforts to "save" Dan and thus thwart Uncle Henry's desire to have the useless dog done away with.

a) Describe *three* such incidents in the story and show that the author has made them exciting and suspenseful.

b) In each case, show how Luke temporarily resolves the "problem" involved, and reveals the depth of his character to us.

2. "I can't seem to think of a place to take you," Luke says.

a) In what sense has the original conflict not been resolved?

b) What internal conflict still remains in Luke?

c) From your understanding of Uncle Henry, do you think he *can* give in to Luke? Are the conflicts worse or better at this point in the story? Explain.

3. In a paragraph, describe your feelings at this point in the story. (Refer to the actions and emotions created by the author). What would you do if *you* were Luke?

LESSON TWO

– Discuss oral questions. Focus on the nature of the *conflicts*, the role of character and action in intensifying our *interest* in the conflicts, and in directing our emotional responses. Use experiential analogues wherever possible to reinforce this response.

– Have written answers read aloud, compared, and discussed.

HOMEWORK

Reread the conclusion to the story (pp. 63-66). (#4 to be written)

1) How does Mr. Kemp decide to solve an "impractical" problem with a "practical" answer?

2)(a) Describe, in detail, Uncle Henry's reactions to Luke's proposal. What internal conflicts now become evident? How is he able to save face?

(b) Are you sympathetic with Uncle Henry's dilemma here? Why or why not?

3)(a) Show that Luke has kept his vow and "learned" something of value from Uncle Henry.

(b) Do you find this resolution satisfying? Why or why not?

4) "The last paragraph of the story, and its title, point up not only the *real* conflict involved, but suggest a deeper meaning, a moral, which the author wishes to convey to the reader." Write a paragraph in which you illustrate this quotation. If you wish, include some real-life examples which might demonstrate this "deeper meaning".

LESSON THREE

Discuss oral questions. Focus on the resolution of the various conflicts from both a structural and an emotional viewpoint. Direct students toward the *meaning* of the conflict (practical versus sentimental) and then have written answers read and discussed.

FOLLOW-UP

1) Read Morley Callaghan's story "All the Years of Her Life". In your discussion groups, consider the following questions.

    a) Like "Luke Baldwin's Vow", this story is about characters in conflict.

        i) Draw a character sketch of Alfred and of Mrs. Higgins.

        ii) What is Alfred's view of his mother?

        iii)What feelings does she seem to have about her son?

        iv) What are your feelings toward each of them in the first part of the story? At the end?

    b) The plot is also simple in this story, focusing on a single incident and its aftermath. Show how the actions of the plot serve to intensify the problem between Alfred and his mother, and to direct our feelings about the characters.

    c) There is a "moral" in this story as well. What has Alfred learned about himself, his mother, and life in general?

    d) How does the "surprise" ending help the reader to better understand Alfred's problem?
      How does it serve to give this "moral" a powerful *emotional* impact?

    e) Write a paragraph (individually or as a group) in which you explain the central *meaning* of the story. Include references to other real-life situations which might contain a similar meaning.

NOTE:

The close reading of "Luke Baldwin's Vow" should give students the necessary *literary* background to pursue this less structured assignment with some degree of success. Thus, the literary element can be allowed to submerge, so that PERSONAL RESPONSE and EXPERIENTIAL ANALOGUE can be emphasized in an atmosphere of open and free-wheeling discussion.

Further follow-up work can thus be increasingly general without doing essential damage to the literary quality and import of the material. For example:

2) Read Morley Callaghan's story "A Cap For Steve". In your discussion groups, consider the following questions:

(a) "Morley Callaghan's stories often involve a close study of characters in conflict. The plot is often simple, but the emotions and desires of the characters are always complex. The story often ends with the characters gaining some insight into the meaning of their lives, an insight shared by the reader who has glimpsed, for a moment, the complex reality of ordinary living." Show to what extent this quotation applies to "A Cap For Steve."

(b) Write a paragraph explaining the central point of this story. Comment on your reactions to Dave, to Steve, and their problem.

3) "Morley Callaghan, in his stories, reveals an understanding of and deep feeling for ordinary people and their problems." Discuss with reference to the three stories studied and any two other stories by the same author.

4) Write a short story which involves an essential conflict of character.

– 06 –

The View from Darien:

The Drama of Literature in the Classroom

— Part 1

The English Quarterly XV, 1 (Spring 1982)

On reading John Dixon's book **Education 16-19: the Role of English and Communication**[1] I was struck once again by the unanimity of aims among those who profess to teach literature to high school students. In Part II Dixon is describing the goals of a group of concerned English teachers in the U.K., and their statements are both predictable and happily familiar. After noting such general experiential aims as "an understanding of the human state", "an awareness … of their own experience and that of others," and "an appreciation of mature ideas and feelings maturely expressed … to make them their own", Dixon's colleagues note these specific hopes for literature teaching: Teaching literature involves helping students to make the best of such **encounters** (*with texts*) by: (*italics mine*)

— (*giving*) students more confidence in their approach to previously unknown texts

— (*broadening*) the range of writers a student can meet with heightened expectation

— (*giving*) students some ideas of the ways into any book that seems alien or puzzling

— (*having students*) aim for an active tolerance which senses qualities in literature they do not greatly care for as well as that which they do enjoy … and to realize why this is so (*Coleridge's "willing suspension of disbelief"*).

— (*developing*) the ability to entertain visions of life and perspectives on it that are initially alien (*which depends on*) the people we respect and our feeling for the language they use

— (*having them*) read carefully and thoroughly, with sensitivity to emotion and tone

— (*developing*) discrimination and judgment … a feeling … for values

— (*having them*) use a growing critical faculty of what they read or see and rely on their own judgment in matters of criticism

— (*making them aware of*) craft to enable one's appreciation to be deepened

— (*having them*) appreciate the relation of form to content

— (*studying*) texts in the context of their time and cultural background[2]

Teachers on this side of the Atlantic will nod appreciatively. We may even accept the claim Dixon makes that these were goals the teachers felt they could achieve, and indeed had achieved from time to time in spite of a rigid external examination system.[3]

Although much else has changed (the subject of Dixon's book), our hopes for literature have remained constant, as they should. We have suffered from no scarcity of clearly elaborated goals —rooted in criticism, aesthetics, linguistics, language development theory, and long experience in the classroom. Neither do we find any dearth of course descriptions, syllabi, book lists, and rationales for particular approaches. What we do lack is a *general* account of what happens in a high school English class when literature is being taught, and in particular when it is being taught towards the ends mentioned above.

When the teacher closes his door, takes out a text, and starts talking with his students, how does he arrange for them to encounter the poem or story, to participate in its vicarious experience, to hold the disbelief in check, to develop systematically their own ability to probe more deeply into alien language and form? How is it done? Where would we look to find out? If we check our examinations or essay assignments, we will no doubt find large questions that demand significant response to major texts, perhaps even calling for personal interpretation and social/cultural application. But even when the students have been successful, how did they *learn* to cope with the question, to understand its demands, to break it down into parts, to read the text under its constraints? And, of course, neither examinations nor term papers can fully evaluate the affective, moral, and experiential aspects of our most lofty goals. Nevertheless, at our best, we sense (know?) that sophisticated reading skills are being acquired and significant behavioral change is taking place among our students over the course of a year's instruction. Dixon's associates felt so, and offered their classes and services to the Schools' Council experiments in light of that belief. I accept the notion that in the best classrooms, over there and here in my own region (southwestern Ontario), the major goals are being occasionally achieved. I could take you to the classes and teachers I have in mind. How representative they are of the profession as a whole is a question I cannot answer. The question I would like answered, and intend to address, may ultimately be more important: how does the successful teacher achieve with his students, consistently and systematically, the highest cognitive and affective goals—goals which often seem to be pipe-dreams for many teachers who care but cannot cope? Where do the latter go for help? Without a description of what actually happens in the successful classroom, no restatement of goals, new guidelines, study-guides or "teacher-proof" package will do.

Quite often we approach the problem of describing the particular dynamic of the literature class by looking at what we feel to be the most obvious variables: the teacher's "personality" (high-key/low-key, dramatic/boring, caring/aloof); the teacher's "style" (open/structured, demanding/undemanding); the methodology (Socratic, group discussion, tutorial, heuristic, recitation); the course of study; the mix of students; the atmosphere of the school (philistine, scholarly, permissive); and so on. No one would deny the significance of any of these, and yet none defines what is peculiar to the English class when a poem or novel is being successfully encountered and explored. The "best" classrooms that Professor Dixon and I have in mind exist among these variables, willy-nilly, and while one set of them may support and facilitate an effective program (and ought therefore to be promoted), it nonetheless will not form the crucial set of factors. Looked at another way, the question becomes: even if all the secondary variables listed above were favorable, would the goals of our literature program be automatically achieved? If the teacher were in a scholarly atmosphere, with carefully streamed advanced students, with texts of his own choosing in sufficient quantities, with a repertoire of methods delivered in a dramatic, open, democratic spirit and set in a heuristic context of exploration and discovery—would the students learn to read, suspend disbelief, and make meaningful connections? Probably they would, but we have no guarantee of success here; some teachers will still fail. The primary elements of effective literature teaching have not yet been isolated, nor has their fundamental dynamic.

What follows is a first attempt to delineate these elements as they are practised by the best teachers I know of. We will look at the elements in action, for their relationship can only be described through the metaphor of drama. We will keep them as free as possible from the secondary variables though these, in reality, impinge at all points. The purpose in doing so is not to ignore the latter but rather to make their role in the teaching process clearer when seen in the light of the former. Teaching can only be improved when first principles have been rightly considered. Teachers may legitimately complain about "tight budgets" but financial restraint is not the *prime* reason for Mary's failure to read *Macbeth* with competence and interest.

The account to follow is not strictly representative, even of my own private sample: in all cases the reality has been idealized to form a composite working model. All the teachers whose labor and talent I have used to derive the model would, I am confident, recognize it as roughly descriptive of "the kind of thing I do," though the weighing of elements and the priorities among goals would bear their personal stamp. The secondary variables would further distort any model that purports to be primary. Yet the elements I will describe are primary, necessary, and prerequisite. What I hope to discover by delineating them is how far the model is recognizable beyond these provincial borders, among those hundreds of teachers, like Dixon's colleagues, who harbor common ideals. Can we begin trading secrets?

The literature lesson has three primary and interacting elements: a teacher, a text and students. The teacher, as mature/model reader and author's surrogate, raises questions out of the text; the students, as apprentice readers but full-fledged responders, "answer" the questions and in doing so are brought into close contact with the text in a context of peer response and adult supervision. The result is that students learn to read increasingly sophisticated texts (1) *initially* by listening to peers answer the questions, participating in group response to the questions, and/or answering them independently, and (2) *over the long term* by appropriating the questions, consciously and unconsciously, abstracting their general features and applicability, and bringing them to bear on new texts. Moreover, and at the same time, these questions, governed by the teacher's presence as mature/model reader and by the class/group/individual response, will direct students to the affective, moral, and experiential aspects of literature.

These statements constitute a pedagogical dynamic and a theory of learning-to-read literature. These elements must be present (I'm hypothesizing, of course) and must be set in special relation to one another. The questions which quicken and sustain the drama among the teacher, text, and students must be of a kind and structure to promote cognitive, affective, moral, and experiential (social, cultural) goals in specific instances and over a period of time[4]; and the texts themselves must be appropriately selected in light of the above.

We will now examine the separate parts of the model. First the teacher must be a *mature, model reader*, that is, he should himself be free from the major reading fallacies and prejudgments inimical to our accepted goals. Intentionalism, affectivism, literalness, allegorizing—these must be purged.[5] Suspension of the disbelief and the development of negative capability can hardly be inculcated by a teacher who holds a single-minded (bloody-minded?) view of Emily Dickinson's "Because I Could Not Stop For Death." Nor can the patient exploration of this subtle poem be encouraged by off-hand but otherwise clever remarks like "What do you expect from her, cooped up like that for thirty years?" I'm exaggerating here (I hope), but the point is that, in general, we must take stock of our own habitual behavior as readers, a role we play in public before our students every day. The relevance of literature, the connectedness that students will come to see over time between the texts and the life in them and around them—these major goals will be achieved not merely through intelligent bridging questions but also by the model (as reader and responder) provided by the teacher day in and day out.

Frank Smith defines the teacher's role this way[6]:

A reader "gets the meaning" of a book or poem from the writer's (or a teacher's) point of view only when the reader asks questions that the writer (or teacher) implicitly expected to be asked... A particular skill of writers (and of teachers), based usually on exceptional experience, understanding and sensitivity, is to lead a reader to ask the questions that they consider appropriate.

The teacher, in the absence of the author, is the defender of the integrity of the text. He best fulfills this role by raising questions the author himself would wish to have raised, commensurate with the capabilities of the students for whom the text has been selected. The form of these questions, though, is a *pedagogical* decision: Emily Dickinson would want the reader to respond to the irony, word-play, and image patterns of her poem as they develop and convey her feelings about death, but the decision about how best to arrange the presentation of the poem and its questions is the teacher's alone. His success in this regard will be measured by how well the students find that the questions open up the text, encourage student-modified questions, and are compatible with questions of their own; and, most important, to what degree the questions become independent of the teacher as a person, an authority figure and an individual interpreter. Put another way, the questions should bring the student progressively into a close and genuine encounter with the text: they should not draw him prematurely away from it nor provide an impenetrable barrier between text and responder; nor should they interfere with an open response by proffering convenient stock or conventional stances (more on this below).

The position of the text has been indirectly defined in the above account. The text is not inert, something to be "covered" or summarized. It is alive in relation to the teacher who must be perceived to have read it himself in depth and with sensitivity, and whose questions must be finely tuned to its unique desiderata and to the needs of the students. It is alive in relation to the students who must sense that they are encountering it— directly (when teacher intervention is slight or delayed) or indirectly through teacher-mediated questions designed to compel response from the students by turning them towards the text and their own intimations about it.

The student, then, is both apprentice and journeyman. He is an apprentice reader in that there are questions he does not know how to ask about certain texts, consciously or unconsciously. The teacher must ensure that text selection and questions are directed to these needs—his lessons must reflect some emphasis on the systematic development of reading skills, geared where possible to individual requirements. On the other hand, *no student is ever an apprentice responder*. Such an assumption (not unknown in the profession) is incompatible with our generally held goals. The students will like or dislike, react deeply or shallowly, sense the implications of a symbol or no, relate the theme to their social milieu or ignore the connection, feel morally superior to the hero or be awed by his circumstance—these kinds of responses are subject to no apprenticeship. (There is, of course, a steady development here as students mature from grade nine to twelve, but while they always *know* they are apprentice readers to some extent, they should not *feel* like apprentice responders: at a given moment, what they feel or can tolerate or how much disbelief they can suspend is complete and "real": we do not want them feigning these values to conform to our expectations; advanced reading skills, on the other hand, can't be faked.) Students' values and feelings, then, are genuine and unique to each occasion. The teacher who lets his personal interpretation and/or his questions interfere with an open response to the legitimate, affective aspects of literature is erecting a roadblock between student and text, reader and self. As reading instructor, the teacher has duties and responsibilities which compel him to intervene to ensure an orderly growth in reading competency, but he must be careful not to trample on the equally compelling duty of the student to be himself. These duties overlap, of course, and it is a matter of discrimination and a sense of balance which should govern our actions here. The model calls for an awareness of this complex duality.

Teacher as model reader and author surrogate; a text enlivened by vital questions; students as apprentice readers and genuine responders drawn into an encounter with the text through the mediation of questions—this is the drama which is played out until the plot is moved to the point where the questions have become inseparable from the text itself, now opened up to students who are facing it "on their own." In the best lesson sequences the students will write their own fifth act.

We have looked at the basic elements and said that they play clearly defined roles in relation to one another. Though somewhat fixed, as we have seen, the role of the student and teacher *vis a vis* the text (the stable object in the scene) does nevertheless evolve, moving from an initial pattern through a series of stages, or acts, to some sort of climax and resolution. There is a line of action in this play, determined by a shift in relation between and among the elements. Figure 1 presents the drama in schematic form.

In Act I the teacher reads the text privately as mature reader, asking and answering his own questions (Q1) which lead him to a comprehension as complete as his own training allows. He then selects questions suited to his students and casts them in an appropriate form and sequence (Q2). The students receive these questions, perceiving them initially as *teacher* questions, and read the text by answering them. The teacher intervenes directly and regularly (the arrow from "Text" to "Teacher") by accepting or rejecting answers, redirecting responses (back to the text, to other students, or both) or rephrasing his initial question (Q2 broken down into parts). At this stage the teacher appears in full control of the questions and the adjudication of answers. The students' encounter with the text is very much qualified; they feel like students.

In Act II, the teacher's questions (Q2) still initially control the encounter but, if they are compatible with the text and the student's reading abilities, they will move the student closer to the text because they are, in general, now more familiar. Aspects of the specific text begin to modify the questions in light of the students' ongoing response. Teacher questions (Q2) become enmeshed with the student-reader's own immediate needs (Q3); they appear less oriented to the teacher as teacher, and more relevant to the reading of the text. The teacher's intervention now oscillates from regular to intermittent (dotted arrow from "Text" to "Teacher"), applied as needed, and incorporating both original questions and those modified by the students themselves (Q2/Q3). The students get their first intimations that the teacher may be a reader as well, and that he wants them likewise to be readers.

Figure 1 – Stages in the Teaching and Learning of Literature

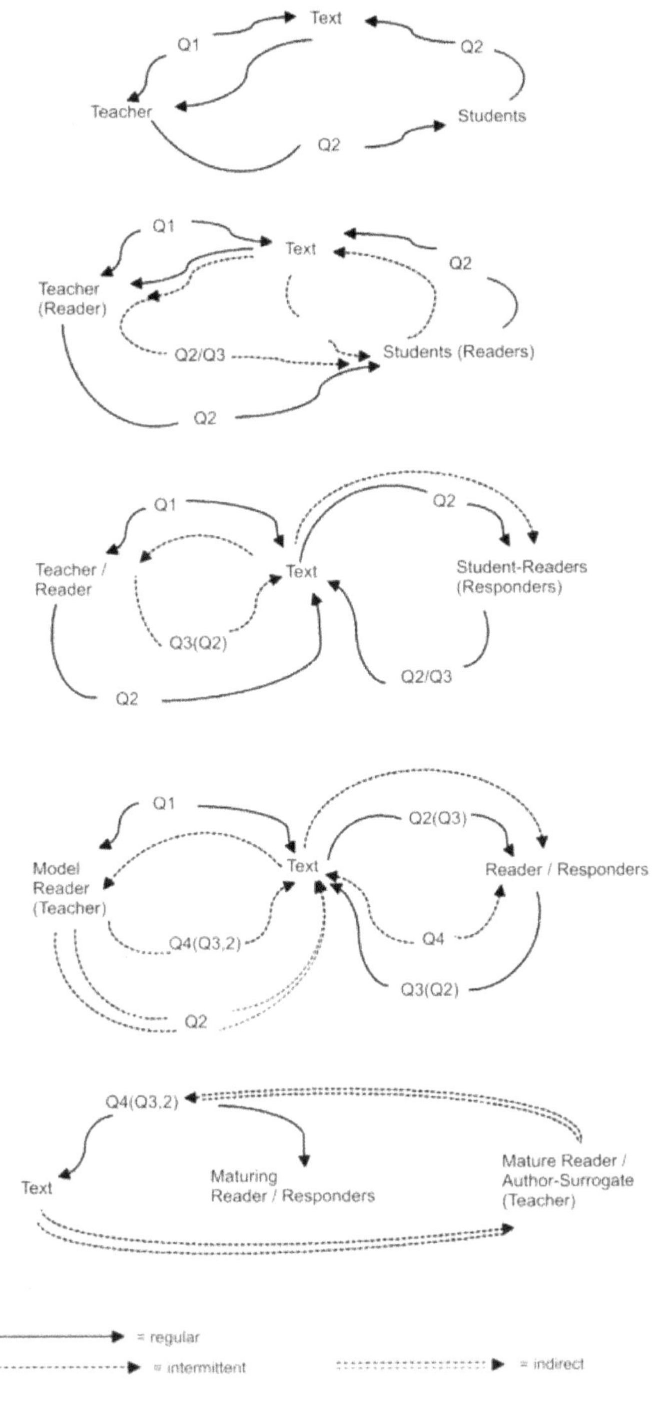

Q1 = questions promoted by and derived from the text by the teacher
Q2 = questions modified by teacher for students
Q3 = teacher-questions modified by students as they encounter the text
Q4 = questions raised by students from the text (and past experience)
Q5 = student-questions modified by teacher when necessary

In Act III a more dramatic shift occurs. The teacher's questions (Q2) are perceived to flow not from him but out of the text to them. The text has assumed a more intermediate position between teacher and student. This shift, though substantial, is one of perception, for the teacher is still asking pedagogical questions (Q2). However, they are now even more familiar in kind and form (though still shaped uniquely to this text), and occasionally a little more general and open-ended. Moreover, the students have gained confidence in them as angles on the text, as instruments to open the text to them. Their past experience allows them at this stage to focus on questions to be answered *vis a vis* the text rather than upon answers to please an interrogating teacher. Hence, more licence is taken by students in modifying teacher questions according to immediate and ongoing response (Q2/Q3). Consonant with this new freedom is the teacher's intermittent intervention which redirects their own modified questions (Q3) back through the text, without, where possible, repetition or rephrasing of initial questions (Q2). The text has been moved downstage; the teacher is both teacher and reader; the students, actively involved in reformulating questions and relying less on the teacher's adjudication, begin to feel more like readers. The answers, more and more, seem to lie in the text and in themselves as readers and responders. A turning point has been reached.

Act IV brings the student-reader face to face with the text itself. The teacher, who has been asking text-specific questions to qualify, direct, sequence and mediate the encounter, has begun to withdraw. He has become the model (mature) reader who arranges the event (selects the text or supervises its selection) and provides an initiating stimulus (a general or conventional question requiring reformulation to apply to a specific text, a challenging critical quotation, a series of large interpretive tasks, etc.). His role as adjudicator is taken up only when necessary, and consists mainly of redirecting the students' reformulated and/or original questions [Q4(Q3,2)] back to the text. Responses are adjudicated *after the event* whenever possible by the teacher as model reader. The students, with only a general framework to qualify their encounter with the text, must create their own specific questions from past experience with teacher questions (Q2 to Q3) and generate their own constituent ones from the immediate encounter and from past reading experience in general (Q4). They are now readers as well as students—applying general questions and composing new ones, and taking more responsibility for assessing their responses.

Act V marks the high point of the drama, creating at once a feeling of intense excitement and one of completion. Students are at last on their own with the text. The teacher may still arrange the event, and even set a task or two, but these actions will be perceived as flowing from a mature reader whose *only* intervention will take place after the event, after the students have had a chance to recast initiating questions and/or raise their own. He will be seen as judging the quality of their questions and their abilities as maturing readers, and as the author's friendly ombudsman. More important, he will be an adult reader who wishes to share in their human responses to the common experience of great literature.

The five acts of stages with their essential elements, then, comprise the primary drama of the high school literature class. The following qualifications should be considered before we examine, in Part II, its ideal structure against the actual school setting and before we assess its usefulness to teaching.

(1) The description of the elements and their interrelation within each stage are not "pure." Glimpses of earlier or later stages will occur within any one of the stages. For example, some direct teacher intervention might take place for brief periods during Stage V without substantially altering the sense that a Stage V enactment is indeed taking place; similarly, the occasional open question might appear in Stage 1 without substantially affecting the students' perception of the teacher's role and the position of the text peculiar to that stage. The stages describe a prevailing pattern of action and an overall set of roles and response-situations. They recount what can happen when a certain paradigm is set in motion; they are descriptive, not prescriptive.

(2) The model is developmental, in stages which are sequential and interdependent, yet self-contained. For example, the position of the text in any stage is determined by the teacher's questions which determine the student's perception of the text which determines his perception of the teacher's role which in turn helps to define his own, etc. Progress, or growth, will be achieved over the long term by the shift (back and forth, up and down) from one stage to another, not from the parts of one stage to the parts of another.

(3) Although each stage is primarily defined by the changing nature of the relations among elements, it is not unimportant to observe the changes within the elements across the grid. Questions tend to move from text-specific to general; teacher intervention from regular to intermittent to *post hoc*; the students' perception of the instructor's role shifts from Teacher all the way to Mature Reader; the student begins as Student and emerges as Maturing Reader/Responder. But it is the inner workings of the drama itself that can best product these changes. The teacher might role-play "Friendly Ombudsman" for a day but he has not necessarily established a learning situation at Stage V.

(4) Not all students in a given class or group will attain competency at the same rate or to the same degree, nor will they reach identical stages on each occasion. Students and teacher, nevertheless, should be aware of the stages that lie ahead, with the ultimate goals always in sight. Some sense of movement or growth is essential at all times. All students should be allowed to experience the whole drama as often as possible.

(5) In this regard, then, the schema does not translate into age or grade equivalents. Grade nines reading a short story will not necessarily require the constraints of teacher-questions at Stage I, nor conversely will grade twelves, because they are more experienced, begin each story at Stage III or IV. "The Rime of the Ancient Mariner" may be successfully encountered by grade tens moving from initial teacher guidance (Stages I to III) to some open-ended response by students working independently in groups; the same poem might be taught in grade twelve, using the whole drama with a different set of tasks given

at each stage. As Frank Smith has pointed out, comprehension *for a student* occurs when *he* has no more of his own questions unanswered.[7] It is the teacher who decides what additional questions are to be asked during the reading encounter.

(6) Hence, the drama itself applies essentially to each occasion when a major text is read in depth: the selection of texts and setting of tasks will determine the pace, emphasis and relative success of the enterprise. The full drama may occur in a single class period (occasionally) or across a series of periods, a unit of work, a term, a course of study or a program. In practice, the minimum period for measuring growth across the full range of competencies and behaviors implied in the model will likely be the unit (three to ten weeks of focused study). Nonetheless, the whole drama could occur in miniature during constituent lessons as well as in general over the duration of the unit. The students' perception of role changes will be for most of them a long-term effect; but it may be the brief glimpses of new roles and competencies *en route* that contribute most to learning.

(7) Though sequential and interdependent, the stages, in daily practice, do not have to be invariably enacted from I to V. During a poetry unit, for example, a lesson on a new poem, somewhere in the middle of the unit, might *begin* with a general question and method (group discussion) that gives students the feeling they are in Stage IV. However, if the students cannot handle the challenge (i.e., cannot break down the general question into appropriate parts *vis a vis* the specific text, or cannot function without regular intervention from the teacher), then the teacher has Stage III to retreat to, not only for the remainder of this lesson, but for the next few lessons in the unit, until he feels the class is ready for a substantive shift to Stage IV. The presence of a developmental, staged model should eliminate the temptation on either side to retreat, in panic, all the way to the safety of Stage I.

The model, whatever the circumstances, is dramatic and dynamic. That is its essential feature. It provides us with an ideal that compels some movement at all times for teacher and students; it puts these demands in sequence to allow teacher and students to feel the real dynamic of learning-to-read-literature; it allows the teacher to teach and the students to learn; it puts the text where it belongs in the English class: at the centre of our attention.

Notes:

[1]John Dixon, *Education: 16-19, The Role of English and Communication* (London: Macmillan, 1979). Dixon reviews the teaching of English in the U.K. from 1945 to the present and comments on current trends.

[2]*Ibid.*, pp. 46-48, rearranged.

[3]*Ibid.*, p. 47.

[4]For a discussion of these goals and the kind of questions needed to achieve them, see Don Gutteridge, "The Major Novel in the Senior Grades," *The English Quarterly*, X, 3 (Fall 1977), pp. 18-22.

[5]See, W.K. Wimsatt, Jr. and Monroe Beardsley, "The Affective Fallacy" and "The Intentional Fallacy", in W.K. Wimsatt, Jr., *The Verbal Icon* (Lexington: The University of Kentucky Press, 1967).

[6]Frank Smith, *Understanding Reading*, rev. ed. (New York: Holt, Rinehart, and Winston, 1978).

[7]*Ibid.*, pp. 66-67

The View from Darien: The Drama of Literature in the Classroom

— Part Two

The English Quarterly XV, 2 (Spring 1982)

So far, the model described in Part One tells us some important things about what goes on in an English classroom when literature is being taught; and these are intimately connected with a set of general goals widely accepted by English teachers. But what happens when an abstract model hits the actual classroom? Can we apply it for very long (at all?) without running head-on into secondary factors like school environments, program design, and teacher idiosyncrasy? Certainly, we must look at the way in which selected secondary factors interact with primary ones; for example, the way in which questions are primary and methodology secondary. We should examine in more detail the principles of question formation as they relate to the realization of our twin goals: developing reading competence and broadening the awareness of the uses of literature. And we can examine more closely how the model itself is designed to foster learning specifically within the context of English studies.

We shall discuss these issues in reverse order. We have already noted that the general *pattern of learning* involved in becoming increasingly competent in reading sophisticated literary texts entails, first of all, students' participation in the responses to questions raised from the text to the point where these questions are "taken over" by students for their own use. What does this mean? How does the model advance such a process? Let us take poetry as an example. Over several years of study the student hears his teachers and fellow students raise questions which are peculiar to the comprehension of and response to poetry. These questions lead him to seek out, put together, and interpret image patterns, repetitions, connected metaphors, symbols, *et al.* The questions have always been put in the context of reading an individual poem, so that their *general* structure can only be abstracted over a period of time and across numerous examples. Such a procedure, implicit in the model, curtails inappropriate direct instruction ("Here is a definition of metaphor and three examples.") The recognition of reading cues peculiar in part to poetry, is, moreover, always achieved during individual and group response, so that no stock response is encouraged ("S-sounds always lend a soft, sibilant quality to a stanza", "Love poems are sentimental"). Students, by participating at various stages in pursuit of answers to the questions, learn for themselves, through inference and abstraction, what the general features of these questions are, what constraints they impose in regard to specific texts and applications, and what use they are to students as readers and persons ("Does the new meaning matter?", "Is it worth the intellectual effort?"). Some questions will sink down and become unconscious (the student responds to patterns quickly and naturally), will be able to be raised easily to consciousness when required, and then reapplied. Some will remain conscious but "shaky" ("Here's a poem, I've got to watch out for image patterns and dominant mood"), calling for more experience and less nervous attention in order to become fully appropriated; others will be unconscious enough to shape an initial response but not deep enough to be raised quickly and surely to explicit elaboration or validation (*e.g.,* the student who gives a fine "narrative" response to a poem but cannot generalize from it, and may not wish to). The foregoing are mere guesses at a complex mental process which every teacher has observed in operation but none of us fully understands. We are concerned here with the pedagogical procedure and circumstance that will foster observable growth in reading literature, whatever its inner workings may prove to be.

However, as a learning process, the business of appropriating questions and using them is fraught with danger. Without a dynamic teaching model to control it, it can easily lead students to make shallow generalizations as they appropriate only stock questions and parrot back stock responses[1] ("We always start with the mood and then look for the sustained metaphor; sonnets rhyme 'abba'," *etc.*). This pedagogical model calls for the teacher to be a mature reader so that his questions will be appropriate to the kind of text under review (sonnet, haiku, concrete poem) and its uniqueness (feelings, ideas, particular language features). Just as important is the role of the question as a way into the poem and not a way out: not "Show how Browning imposed his own values on those of the past" nor "List five qualities of the dramatic monologue and illustrate them from 'My Last Duchess', but rather "What in the Duke's character compelled him to have his wife killed? Listen to the tone of his voice and watch for the things he values." Once asked, the questions belong to the student; they work to open up the poem to further questions, personal responses, shared or disputed views. The teacher chairs the discussion, moves the question forward or back when necessary, redirects his apprentice readers to aspects of language or form that clarify response and interpretation. He adjudicates and intercedes, as the author's proxy, only when significant parts have been overlooked, a pattern drifts unnoticed, or an obstreperous student inflicts a seriously fallacious reading on his captive peers. The teacher provides no answers and no notes except, on occasion, a record of student responses. As model reader he begins to nudge the class towards a wider application of their responses: "How do you feel about the Duke? Are there people like him about you now? Did you sympathize at all? What makes people become like that? Othello killed the woman *he* loved, too; did he have anything in common with the Duke?" And so on.

This latter kind of questioning illustrates how the parts of the pedagogical model–teacher/text/students–interact to provide a continuous, balanced and dynamic "drama" which allows students to learn the skills and processes of reading literature while at the same time learning its uses, constraints, and pleasures. Indeed, it is the *questions* which are crucial to the smooth functioning of the model. Elsewhere I have discussed in some detail what I mean by the term "question"[2]; however, a thoroughgoing analysis of the nature of literary questions designed to suit the model and its related goals is a proper study of its own. The examples given above will, I hope, give some indication of the kind of issues involved in question making. It may suffice here to note that the term "question" is being used to cover a range of explicit and implicit types. Put oversimply, questions may be immediate or remote, direct or indirect, student- or teacher-initiated, personal or impersonal, given in advance or delayed, text-specific or conventional, highly or lightly structured, *etc*. At their best they address form and content, skills and uses, comprehension and response as unvarying complements.

From learning process and questions, we come to the third issue: the way in which questions derived from the text by the teacher as mature reader are a primary element in the unfolding drama. Normally we think that the methodology we use is at least as elementary as the questions raised by, say, "My Last Duchess." Surely the decision to employ the so-called Socratic method–where the teacher asks key questions, adjudicates responses, redirects, rephrases, *etc*.–comes before we discover the questions to serve its ends? Not so, at least not in this model. For the reader's (teacher's) first questions, prompted by his encounter with the text, will not necessarily have taken any pedagogical shape, will not yet have been modified by him for his particular class. They remain reader's questions–pure though not simple. For "My Last Duchess", such questions might begin this way: "Who is this strange aristocrat rationalizing the murder of his wife? To a silent (is he?) envoy? (An *envoy*?) What strange asides he makes! Why this obsession with objects of art? Why did he kill her?" And so on. From these first questions we build, still as reader, to some overriding general ones: there seems to be a drama here, with one voice and the felt presence of a second character; and further, a world-view, a past conflict of values unfolding in the "present." Now as teachers we wish our students to encounter the text in some such manner that essential questions are triggered and responded to. We hope we know what some of those questions are, though any response to them must be the student-reader's own responsibility. It is *at this point*, knowing our students as readers and spirited individuals, that we begin to mediate our mature-reader questions, to turn them towards a specific shape and design in order to set up under our jurisdiction an encounter between text and student. If we decide *then* on a Socratic lesson, we may begin to sequence the questions, focus on selected parts of the text, break larger tasks down into manageable units, and think ahead to troublesome student-readers or recurring class problems in poetry analysis. We plan our lesson. In this case the lesson, being Socratic, is itself composed of questions, presented orally and discussed. We may, however, decide that some of our first questions could be provoked from the students by other means. In order to get at the drama in Browning's poem and its monologue form, we might start with a vigorous reading and merely ask the class to discuss, among themselves, the "character" they hear, the "play" going on, and its main conflicts. We might dramatize the poem, with two students or student and teacher playing the two "roles" (rehearsed). Such a presentation by itself calls forth questions, ones the students themselves may be ready to articulate in their own way. Students could be put into their groups and asked only one question: "Why did the Duke murder his wife?"—they approach the problem from the point of view of a team of detectives. In short, *methodology in literature teaching is essentially the mediation of mature-reader questions for a specific group of apprentice readers.*

As such, it follows and flows comfortably out of a knowledge of text and student. It includes the specific use of first questions, their format (oral/written, prior/ongoing/*post hoc*) and their pedagogical setting (Socratic discussion, group discussion, tutorial, dramatic presentation, *et al.*), among other factors. Methodology is as important as first questions, but it is not applied prior to their formation. When it is, then the teacher is less likely to read as a model reader and to enjoy the poem for its own sake and his own; he may more easily fall into the trap of asking stock questions; and he is almost certain to weaken his role as model reader and author surrogate, which in turn blunts or distorts the encounter between text and student—the factor essential to the achievement of our highest aims.

Of what use is a dramatic model for teaching literature? Even if it does describe in a general manner the way in which some of our most successful lessons happen? Even if its elements are primary? A dramatic model serves to facilitate the evaluation of individual programs. Once it is clear that a given department has accepted the major aims suggested at the beginning of this paper, then instead of using the crude testing instruments now available (state-sponsored examinations, school tests and essays, standardized reading tests, subjective observation) evaluation could be based as well on an acceptable *general model* designed to promote the goals. Without such a model (or any model), evaluation of a program must rely on an analysis of test results, a critique of text selection and organization, and personal anecdotal reports by supervisors, where secondary and even trivial factors may predominate (an inspector recently criticized a young teacher for "writing across the cracks on the blackboard"). The dramatic model will allow us to use all these conventional instruments and to set them within a long-term observation of the actual classroom where the teacher/text/student paradigm becomes the framework for analysis.

How would this work? If we monitored an appropriate sequence or selected set of lessons, we could watch for the habitual behaviour of the students in relation to the text: are they more interested in copying notes than in coping with questions, listening to peer response, and modifying or composing questions? Do the teacher's questions move the students prematurely away from the text to "issues" or "opinions"? Do the questions promote a relaxed exploration of the text? No mere test, examination or term paper can ever evaluate these behavioral goals that we write into our curriculum, yet often dismiss because they cannot be "tested", because only the teacher really knows anyway, because after all if students can read technically (whatever that is), then they *are* readers and the rest will happen naturally. Both the goals we have agreed upon and the nature of the reading act itself exclude the latter rationalizations. For reading literature involves more than recognizing symbols or spotting "significant detail"; conversely, learning to "love" it entails a discriminating response to its language as well as its themes and private pleasures. The purpose of the model as an evaluation instrument is to ensure that a primary pattern of teaching/learning is indeed occurring, one devised in its structure and movement to foster growth in reading as we have defined it.

We could also watch for the relation of teacher to text: does the teacher insist on a single interpretation, usually his own? (Even if it is a valid one, and even if the students accept it graciously, such behavior runs counter to the learning-mode of the model). Is he interested in the text as a mature and model reader? Perhaps the text selection has been made without his consent and has been ill-chosen for both instructor and students. At this point an important secondary curriculum factor impinges naturally upon a primary behaviour. In similar ways, matters of methodology could be analysed in light of their compatibility with the model. A program well-conceived in terms of goals, text selection and teacher commitment to role may be observed rarely to move the students beyond Stage III. Lack of skill in handling group discussion or setting up independent study may prove to be the weak spot in the design. Methodology *per se* need never be considered in isolation; the teacher who uses his own devices to create the dynamic and effect, say, of Stage IV will not have to apologize for or change them. Whatever the idiosyncrasies and accidents of particular classrooms or text selections or favorite approaches (themes, genres), the observer should be left with a set of general and consistent impressions: that the students are moving surely towards some independence and are encountering the texts more and more directly, with accompanying challenges, healthy uncertainties and well-earned confidence. Whatever the course, method or style, the program is working.

Certainly, if our current *ad hoc* arrangements for teacher evaluation are left unencumbered by more primary considerations, the present inequities will continue to prevail. Teachers become rightly defensive in the face of new guidelines formulated by someone else and demanding instant changes–in methods (group discussion is the latest "fad") and program (more listening and speaking, lots of "personal reading"). Neither side has any common and general reference to fall back on. If, on the other hand, we can link general pedagogy to general goals, then we can intervene from the outside to help young teachers or those veterans seeking renewal; most teachers could evaluate their own performance against a trusted set of first principles. If we must intercede from outside, then we can do so at the easiest point of entry–the sequence of daily lessons with its attendant "planning" and performance features. We can do so with as little initial recourse to secondary factors as possible–those aspects of style, personality and pedagogical legerdemain that ought not to be tampered with so long as the primary drama is functioning well.

In evaluating himself, for example, an individual teacher could assess whether the basic relationship among the parts–teacher/text/students–has been achieved even in a Stage I situation. Does the teacher accept his role definition? Do his questions advance it even when he is in regular control (Stage I)? If so, then he may look ahead to Stages II and III to see whether he might extend his basically sound approach to induce more rapid growth in student independence. Perhaps it may be a matter of broadening the range of his methods to suit Stages II and III, or learning more about framing tasks that initiate student-centred exploration of texts, and so on. Conversely, the teacher may be under the illusion that he is enacting Stage IV or V, with lots of group discussion and independent projects, but has not seen the necessity of preparing students by arranging for more experience at Stages I to III, or has not realized the special demands of general questions at advanced stages.[3] Once the goals and model have been accepted, then the stages and parts can be used diagnostically, and their relation to secondary factors (say, text selection or some training in group dynamics) considered in a useful context.

Surely a discussion of whether a teacher's conventional questions are promoting reading skills or whether his reluctance ever to set the text free from his close supervision is stifling his students' response–surely these are more productive points of contention– even when inconclusive–than our squabbling over whether group discussion is a waste of time or textual analysis is boring. The issues involved here are of a different order than we have often assumed: the latter can only be addressed when the former have been thought through. Without a governing model of some kind we are left with our squabbles and prejudices. The dramatic model I have outlined herein is merely a trial run, a step into uncharted waters, a sort of wild surmise from Darien's peak. Keats, and our students, are worth the risks we must take.

Notes:

[1] For a discussion of stock responses, see Don Gutteridge, "The Affective Fallacy and the Student's Response to Poetry", *English Journal, LXI, 2* (February 1972), pp. 210-221. Also discussed are interpretative problems related to over-literalness and wild allegorizing. The teacher's role in inducing reading fallacies is further dealt with in Don Gutteridge, "The Hidden Meaning Syndrome", *The English Quarterly*, IX, 1 and 2 (Spring/Summer 1976), pp. 29-35.

[2] Don Gutteridge, "The Question of English: Toward a General Methodology", *The English Quarterly*, VII, 2 (Summer 1974), pp. 87-103.

[3] Examples of challenging overview questions useful for group exploration or independent study are to be found in James French, ed. *Journeys II* (for grades nine and ten) and Ian Underhill, ed., *Family Portraits* (for grade twelve), both texts in the series *Casebooks in Canadian Literature* (Toronto: McClelland and Stewart, 1978/1979).

– 07 –

The Affective Fallacy

and the Student's Response to Poetry

English Journal LXI, 2 (February, 1972)

The publication of W. K. Wimsatt's "The Intentional Fallacy" and "The Affective Fallacy" in the *Sewanee Review* in 1946 was an important landmark in the history of literary criticism. And while both essays contain significant implications for the teacher as well as the critic, it is "The Affective Fallacy" which modern teachers of literature–and especially of poetry–should now re-examine with some care. For it is the area of affective response which has begun to raise many new problems in the classrooms of contemporary North America.

Many of our current dilemmas are probably a result of the increased permissiveness of a society which puts few demands (mental or physical) on its children, a society in which the term *discipline* can only be used by faculty members susurrating timidly behind closed doors. It is also because of the contemporary phenomenon of popularism in the arts: where the teenager is begged to indulge his emotions in the atavistic rhythms of acid rock; or sip leisurely at the predigested and commercially packaged song-poems of Rod McKuen; or, if he musters courage enough to confront poetry at all, to take it in diluted doses–in the communal security of a coffeehouse or the private safety of a marijuana-dream. This is not to deny the valid claims that can be made for genuine folk-art, rock music, *etc.*, but I have seen no evidence in working with present-day students that they are able to discriminate any better among these forms than they are in the heady world of "high-literature." We would be foolish and not-a-little reckless to believe that the current interest in these popular forms of art has made the job of teaching genuine poetry any easier. Wimsatt, with surprising clairvoyance, seems to have predicted much of what has happened since 1946, because the affective response to art has come to form the dominant critical framework of our age–a *cause célèbre* for the New Left, and a sacred cow for the unwitting young.

What are the ramifications for the classroom of this overemphasis on the affective response? They are a familiar litany to every English teacher. "But that's how *I* feel about this poem, and I don't care much how you or any of the others feel." "What right have you to interfere with my personal interpretation?" "It's what the words mean to me that's important–not anyone else." "I don't like love poems (religious poems, war poems, *etc.*)

at all; why should I read this one? They're all the same!" "I only like poems that have a *theme* to them, themes that are about things now." One could, alas, go on, but these few examples should suffice to point up the relationship between the general pattern of popular culture and art, and our own classrooms. The sad truth is that we cannot avoid these questions (and *should* not avoid them), because art itself, and particularly poetry, "confronts" them by its very nature. On the other hand, modern teachers need answers for these questions, answers that will be satisfying to this new breed of students and at the same time true to the rigorous demands which the best poetry makes upon us all.

As I suggested at the outset, some very clear answers are to be found in Wimsatt's "The Affective Fallacy," despite the hoary irrelevance of its age (1946). Wimsatt makes, among others, two basic points about the nature of poetry. I will discuss these separately, and then illustrate how they may be used in our day-to-day classroom activities.

First, Wimsatt says that poetry does not affect us in the same way that real objects do, and thus cannot be measured in the same affective terms.

Poetry is characteristically a discourse about both emotions and objects, or about the emotive quality of objects. The emotions correlative to the objects of poetry become a part of the matter dealt with—not communicated to the reader like an infection or disease, not inflicted mechanically like a bullet or knife wound, not administered like a poison, not simply expressed as by expletives or grimaces or rhythms, but presented in their objects and contemplated as a pattern of knowledge. Poetry is a way of fixing emotions or making them more permanently perceptible when objects have undergone a functional change from culture to culture, or when as simple facts of history they have lost emotive value with loss of immediacy.[1]

The key phrase here is that poetry is about the "emotive quality of objects" and not about objects in and for themselves as they would normally be perceived and responded to in our everyday life. We can, Wimsatt implies, measure the effects of a disease, say, on humans with some degree of empirical certainty (the patient occasionally dies), but one would not use the same measuring stick to determine a personal reaction to Blake's "Sick Rose." Northrop Frye puts it another way when he says "however useful literature may be in improving one's imagination or vocabulary, it would be the wildest kind of pedantry to use it directly as a guide to life."[2] Poetry is in its truest sense a contemplation of objects in which their interrelationship as understood by the poet is embodied in the artefact itself; the effect on the reader contemplating such an artefact is usually his apprehension of the felt quality of the objects. This idea is by now commonplace, having been fully elaborated by writers like Susanne K. Langer (*Feeling and Form*) and Archibald MacLeish (*Poetry and Experience*). However, it cannot be elaborated too vehemently in an age when art has become—for some—a blatant form of propaganda (some folk-songs of the Peace Movement, action theater, so-called documentary novels, *etc.*). It is in this light that many of our students come to the poetry of contemplation, the poetry of feeling (as opposed to the stimulus response pattern of its more emotional and popular forms), the poetry which preserves the quality of emotion in its time of all time. Wimsatt makes this point abundantly clear in speaking of *Macbeth* as dramatic poetry *vis à vis* Macbeth as historical man.

The murder of Duncan by Macbeth, whether as history of the eleventh century or chronicle of the sixteenth, has not tended to become the subject of a Christmas carol. In Shakespeare's play it is an act difficult to duplicate in all its immediate adjuncts of treachery, deliberation, and horror of conscience. Set in its galaxy of symbols—the hoarse raven, the thickening light, and the crow making wing, the babe plucked from the breast, the dagger in the air, the ghost, the bloody hands—this ancient murder has become an object of strongly fixed emotive value (p. 38).

The value of poetry as a *fixed* pattern of feeling, a permanent set of relationships among objects—rendered through word, rhythm, sound, drama—is easily lost sight of in the hysterical climate of modern-day North America. Nevertheless, we must, as teachers, sympathize with the honest dilemmas of the young as they struggle to make compatible the conflicting aims which they find between the pseudo-art of the streets and the political platform, and that to be found in the valid poetry of past and present as it is elaborated in the classroom.

The only honest way of dealing with this dilemma on the part of our students is to face the problem directly. They will never understand poetry until they see what it *is* and what it is *not*. And they will never learn to assess the depth of their own response until they learn how it works, and works on them. In this regard, Wimsatt provides us with another clue.

It is a well known but nonetheless important truth that there are two kinds of real objects which have emotive quality, the objects which are the reasons for human emotion, and those which by some kind of association suggest either the reasons or the resulting emotion: the thief, the enemy, or the insult that makes us angry, and the hornet that sounds and stings somewhat like ourselves when angry; the murderer or felon, and the crow that kills small birds and animals or feeds on carrion and is black like the night when crimes are committed by men. The arrangement by which these two kinds of emotive meaning are brought together in a juncture characteristic of poetry is, roughly speaking, the simile, the metaphor, and the various less clearly defined forms of association (p. 36).

Metaphor is the way of poetry, simply because it does by its nature establish relationships and provide an emotive penumbra of meaning. In doing so, it renders the quality of its objects in a form to be felt and contemplated, but not to be acted upon, as Frye has warned us. Wimsatt goes on to illustrate this point in reference to *Macbeth*:

These distinctions bear a close relation to the difference between historical statement which may be a reason for emotion because it is believed (Macbeth has killed the king) and fictitious or poetic statement, where a large component of suggestion (and hence metaphor) has usually appeared. The first of course seldom occurs pure, at least not for the public eye. The coroner or the intelligence officer may content himself with it. Not the chronicler, the bard, or the newspaperman. To these we owe more or less direct words of value and emotion (the murder, the atrocity, the wholesale butchery) and all the repertoire of suggestive meanings which here and there in history—

with somewhat to start upon–a Caesar or a Macbeth–have created out of a mere case of factual reason for intense emotion a specified, figuratively fortified, and permanent object of less intense but far richer emotion (p. 37).

He is saying here that our reaction to a real murder might be more intense than our reaction to Macbeth's killing of Duncan. Perhaps we could even measure its effects on us: revulsion, vomiting, intervention, lynching, a street riot. But our response to the murder in the play is surely entailed by the complex emotive quality surrounding the event. We might even consider or feel like lynching someone as a result, but it is always, in true art, a *feeling*, a parallel response to the pattern of words and actions in the play itself.

What does all this mean, though, to the beleaguered classroom teacher? Simply, that his students' response to a poem must be measured as a response to the pattern of emotions embodied in it, to the objects as they are qualified by its language. In short, the only meaningful way in which we can measure the effectiveness of the poems we teach is through the way in which our students respond to the words themselves.

This is the second basic point which Wimsatt makes in his essay. If poetry is fundamentally objects seen qualitatively through the medium of language, then critics (and by implication teachers) must learn to discriminate among the kinds of responses which indicate the depth and range of the poem's effect on them.

The critic whose formulations lean to the emotive and the critic whose formulations lean to the cognitive will in the long run produce a vastly different sort of criticism. The more specific the account of the emotion induced by a poem, the more nearly it will be an account of the reasons for emotion, the poem itself, and the more reliable it will be as an   account of what the poem is likely to induce in other–sufficiently informed– readers. It will in   fact supply the kind of information which will enable readers to respond to the poem. It will talk not of tears, prickles, or other physiological symptoms, of feeling angry, joyful, hot, cold, or intense, or of vaguer states of emotional disturbance, but of shades of distinction and relation between objects of emotion. It is precisely here that the discerning literary critic has his insuperable advantage over the subject of the laboratory experiment and over the tabulator of   the   subject's responses. The critic is not a contributor to statistically countable reports about the poem, but a teacher or explicator of meanings. His readers, if they are alert, will not be content to take what he says as testimony, but will scrutinize it as teaching (p. 34).

These are wise and, in the light of developments since 1946, prophetic words. Practically, they imply that we must insist that our students give specific responses to the poem's word-structure, and the more comprehensive such concrete responses are, the closer we come to being truly affected by the poem. Note that Wimsatt is *not* recommending a cold critical/rhetorical analysis of a poem in and for itself. Nevertheless, it is only through our complete response to the total artefact that a poem can affect us– emotionally and intellectually. If our students are moved to tears, it will be because they responded to the poem's feeling, and not because they are bringing to it the kind of stock-response inherited from the more crass forms of popular art. It is not the tears which the teacher can measure, but rather the impact of the poem (as word-structure) which induced the tears.

But how do we distinguish between literary and crocodile tears? There are no easy answers here, but I have been suggesting thus far that we must *learn* to distinguish, or give over the whole business of teaching poetry. (There are signs that the latter is beginning to happen, in universities as well as high schools.) The cause is not hopeless, though, for two general guidelines present themselves after a close reading of Wimsatt (and Frye, Langer, MacLeish, *etc.*).

First, we must *teach* poetry. We must ask questions not only about its content, but about its structure. We must demonstrate—daily—that close reading will produce in-depth responses that the student will recognize as emotional, as a feeling which he should find quite distinct in kind from his stock-response to popular art (intense as that might be). It should be noted here that Wimsatt makes a clear distinction between intensity of response and richness of response. It may be right here that many of our current pedagogical problems lie, for the adolescent is prone to confuse the two. He may confuse his intense and very genuine response to rock-music or a Rod McKuen poem with the potentially richer and more complex response to Shakespeare or Keats or Shapiro—and thus find the latter wanting. Also, he may find, initially, that his intense reaction to real-life situations—say sexual desire—to be more valid than the "cooler" (to borrow a McLuhanesque term) content of a Shakespearean love-sonnet. Again, we *must* understand and sympathize with these very genuine psychological dilemmas of our youth. And it is only by *teaching* poetry, by showing the student exactly *what it is* and what it can do to him, that he is going to discover its uniqueness and its rightful place among the numerous other emotional responses which make their own genuine demands on him.

A warning is necessary at this point. Many teachers who do attempt to *define* poetry for their students fall into the trap of presenting it in a manner which can only be described as *élitist.* That is, they present it too zealously as the *highest* form of art; they protest too much about its *value* in the hierarchy of emotional response which I have outlined above (valid poetry, valid folk-song, popular "poetry," real-life experiences). Frye also sounds a similar warning about insisting on value-judgments too soon in a literary education: "In my opinion value-judgments in literature should not be hurried. It does a student little good to be told that A is better than B, especially if he prefers B at the time. He has to feel values for himself, and should follow his individual rhythm in doing so" (p. 48).

The result of an elitist approach, which entails value-judgment and often a premature aesthetics of literature, is almost certain to be negative in the contemporary climate. We must, then, teach poetry for what it is and can do, and trust that the student will find for it a proper place in his own life. We must not insist on its superiority over the other legitimate claims made upon his emotional life, even though most of us passionately believe that poetry does induce a higher form of response.

Also, and in spite of my somewhat pejorative remarks about it, we must treat the competing forms of popular poetry and folk-song with deference and tact. One way of handling this delicate matter honestly is to teach a unit of popular poetry or folk-song–in an attempt to demonstrate to students what these forms *are* and what they can *do*, and to show them that some discrimination within these separate modes is possible. The essential point is that the student be made aware in definitional terms that these are unique modes, just as poetry and drama and the novel are. Each makes its own demands and produces its own peculiar effects. Similarly, one can deal with the propagandistic and activist-oriented forms of literature as experiments at the periphery of art, operating from different premises and striving for different goals. If we truly believe in the power of poetry (and we should note here that contemporary poetry, fiction, and drama of high quality is still being written within the traditional conceptual framework of literature), then we will honestly allow it to compete with its newer adversaries or complements in a classroom atmosphere characterized by freedom of inquiry, disciplined analysis, and genuine response. It is conceivable that in the long run we may lose the battle. But surely this is a less despairing thought than to contemplate the present situation, where, in the name of a factitious relevance or a fashionable but muddle-headed interdisciplinary approach, we see English lessons degenerate into debates on pollution or general discussions of sex and life (worthy as these might be in their own right). The decision to teach rests squarely on the shoulders of the individual teacher in his own classroom; and no amount of rationalizing about present cultural conditions will alter the fact.

The first guideline, then, for dealing with the student who says "I can make it mean what I want it to mean" or "I prefer Rod McKuen because he's easier to read and he really *says* something to me" is to teach poetry within a definitional framework which will permit an honest discussion of other forms of art and pseudo-art, and at the same time will allow the student himself to assess its affective value in competition with his other emotional needs and responses. The second guideline, also implied in Wimsatt, is that the teacher must establish a system by which both he and his students can measure response to poetry of all kinds. In short, we must find a way of measuring emotional response which obviates the necessity of our having to count the student's tears or guffaws, or resorting to what Wimsatt sardonically refers to as the "psychogalvanic reflex." Only one avenue is open to the teacher, for he can never know, let alone measure, the real effect of a poem on the student; *e.g.*, how it affects him unconsciously or at the level of feeling below or beyond expression. We can never know in a valid way how much the personal experience of the individual reader colors his responses. (A student whose father had just died would certainly have a peculiar reaction to a poem on death like "Do Not Go Gentle into that Good Night".) Both of these areas are part of every reader's response to poetry, and they are necessary. Unfortunately, they are not measurable, even though every perceptive teacher observes them daily in his students, and no doubt uses them as general tools to gauge the overall effect of his literature program. But these deeply felt, personal responses to individual poems do not help either teacher or student to distinguish the kind and quality of feeling which is unique to poetry. The recently bereaved child, for example, is probably not discriminating between the poet's unique reaction to his father's death and his own reaction to an intensely felt real-life experience. Not that he should or can on this occasion; I am merely trying to emphasize that there are dangerous waters to be crossed when purely psychological or physiological responses are used to measure the affective impact of poetry.

Although we can never disregard the erratic, fortuitous, and genuine responses of the kind outlined above, we can devise a more valid and systematic method of helping students measure their own response to poetry. We can let them talk about the poem and/or write down their reactions to it. In this way they are using words of their own to indicate their response to what it is—essentially—an artefact of words. From their own verbal responses we can at least begin to make a rough but consistent assessment of their more general response—one which will permit us to demonstrate to them what poetry is and is not, how it creates an emotive quality of objects which distinguishes it from experiential objects and from the more direct but less exact emotions of folk-song. Wimsatt gives one example which clarifies this idea of using words to measure the effects of words:

It is not always true that the emotive and cognitive forms of criticism will sound far different. If the affective critic (avoiding both the physiological and the abstractly psychological form of report) ventures to state with any precision what a line of poetry does—as "it fills us with a mixture of melancholy and reverence for antiquity"—either the statement will be patently abnormal or false, or it will be a description of what the meaning of the line is: "the spectacle of massive antiquity in ruins." Tennyson's "Tears, idle tears," as it deals with an emotion which the speaker at first seems not to understand, might be thought to be a specially emotive poem. "The last stanza," says Brooks in his recent analysis, "evokes an intense emotional response from the reader." But this statement is not really a part of Brooks' criticism of the poem—rather a witness of his fondness for it. "The second stanza"—Brooks might have said at an earlier point in his analysis—"gives us a momentary vivid realization of past happy experiences, then makes us sad at their loss." But he says actually: "The conjunction of the qualities of sadness and freshness is reinforced by the fact that the same basic symbol—the light on the sails of a ship hull down—has been employed to suggest both qualities." The distinction between these formulations may seem slight, and in the first example which we furnished may be practically unimportant. Yet the difference between translatable emotive formulas and more physiological and psychologically vague ones—cognitively untranslatable—is theoretically of the greatest importance (pp. 33-34).

Brooks has not only felt the sadness in Tennyson's poem, but by describing that sadness in terms of the poem's metaphor and structure, he indicates a level of response which is emotionally profound and at the same time true to the nature of the poem itself. His response is "cognitively translatable," and hence amenable to some kind of measurement.

In classroom terms, this method of evaluating student response makes two demands on the teacher. He must, of course, have read and understood the poem *qua* poem in order to be able to assess various levels of student response. And secondly, he must permit his students to respond in the widest possible way to the poem's effects. Any good teacher will have assiduously met the first demand. It is the second one which often leads to a misguided teaching of poetry, for the teacher himself is apt to confuse his own personal interpretation of the poem with the poem itself. That is, he succumbs to the affective fallacy himself, and thus is temperamentally unable to teach the poem in any other way. His questions will tend to direct the students not to the poem as verbal structure, but to the poem as he himself has felt it, both cognitively and affectively, with the latter response the more likely one. This procedure gives rise to the oft-repeated student complaint: "But you're giving us your interpretation of the poem!" I would say that if this charge is a repeated one, recurring over a long period of time, then that teacher is either incompetent or has fallen prey to the very fallacy he is attempting to avoid. Many teachers, in the face of this criticism, resort to the tactics outlined earlier: they give in and let the students "do their own thing," and thus both instructor and instructed go down together into the affective morass of stock-response, undefined emotionalism, specious relevance, and other sordid *et ceteras*.

I am suggesting, in the strongest possible terms, that this is not the way out. The way and the truth and the light is to teach not only the poem as poem, but the poem as poetry. In straightforward terms, this means asking questions about the way the words and the structure are operating. Demand concrete verbal responses at all times (orally and written). Let metaphor work its own mystery on the students, so long as their collective eye is trained on the metaphor and not on *your* response to it or on the other forms of experience they may innocently or maliciously bring with them.

If these two guidelines–teaching poetry within a definitional framework, and establishing a hierarchy of verbal responses to individual works of art–are religiously adhered to, and if the classroom is genuinely imbued with a spirit of democratic but disciplined inquiry, and if the teacher is aware of and sympathetic to the honest confusions of the adolescent, then the results can only be favorable. For the students will see and feel poetry in a light which is clear, defining, and personally illuminative. As Wimsatt's essay implies so cogently, there really are no alternatives. The road is rocky but straight. For better or worse, we must take it.

II

Enough of theory, says the skeptic; what about practice? It is, of course, impossible to illustrate with any degree of adequacy the guidelines discussed in Part I. The variables are almost infinite in any given teaching situation; our critical terminology has not yet been standardized; and the full complexity of poetry and our human response to it can never be described in absolute terms. Nevertheless we write about critical ideas and pedagogical strategies in much the same spirit in which we dare to teach: the spirit of trust. We trust that our ideas will be heard and understood by those who have shared the literary and human experience over a long period of time. Thus, in teaching, we find basic situations which are common, techniques which can be described, and ideas which are comprehensible.

99

In this light, I will not attempt to elaborate on specific classroom procedures for achieving the first guideline outlined in Part I. If the teacher does know what poetry is and how it means, I trust that he will be able to teach it, provided he is aware of the nature, causes, and results of the Affective Fallacy.

However, the second guideline–developing a hierarchical structure of verbal response to poetry–might be illustrated by reference to a single poem, which can serve at least as a reference point for a theory which is obviously complex and demanding of further elaboration. I will refer to a descriptive lyric by Leonard Cohen[3], list some of the possible (and common) kinds of responses which students might give to it. These responses have been deliberately stylized and somewhat exaggerated (I hope), but the practicing teacher will recognize them as types, even though they rarely occur in their purest form.

Here is the poem:

> Go by brooks, love,
> Where fish stare,
> Go by brooks,
> I will pass there.
>
> Go by rivers,
> Where eels throng,
> Rivers, love,
> I won't be long.
>
> Go by oceans,
> Where whales sail,
> Oceans, love,
> I will not fail.

Let us assume that this poem has been given to a class of high school students, in the academic stream of Grade 11 or 12, as a piece of "sight" work. They have been asked merely to express what feelings the poem aroused in them, and to elaborate on these as fully as possible with reference to the text of the poem.

Here are five responses which, I feel, would represent a reasonable cross section from such a class:

1. This is a typical kind of love-poem, with the poet telling his love that he will climb mountains and cross oceans for her. It reminds me of Simon and Garfunkel or Donovan because there is a nice rhythm to it, and the images are about rivers and brooks and lovely pictures of whales, which suggest the dreaminess of love, and how romantic it all is. In fact it all seems a bit too much, for today's kids don't really talk like this when they're in love. Maybe there should be some music added to it. I like Leonard Cohen's songs very much.

2. This is not really a love-poem at all. It is a poem about life. It begins with the childhood stage (brooks) and carries on with the realities of adult life (rivers and eels, suggesting conflict and strife). The last stanza is the fulfillment of life in a life after death, in oceans   where even the whales "sail." This seems to be a Christian poem, and the love here is the love of man for God, and the trust he has in Him to carry his human creation along the waters of life to the eternity of oceans.

3. This is a love-poem. The poet seems to be talking to his girlfriend, and telling her that he will be with her near the brook (maybe a beautiful place where they planned to meet). He also tells her that he will come soon ("I won't be long") and that he will not fail her. They seem to be very much in love, and plan to travel across rivers and oceans. It seems to be an intense love affair. There is a rhyme scheme here, abab, which makes it sound more like a love lyric.

4. This is a very beautiful love-poem. In it we hear the voice of the lover talking to his loved   one. It seems as if she is far away, and he is reassuring her, for he tells her that if she goes "by brooks" he will definitely "pass there." This is emphasized by his use of the word "will." He then tells her that if she goes "by rivers" he will be there too, and to make it more reassuring, he tells her that he "won't be long." In the last stanza he says that even if she goes "by oceans" he "will not fail." All of this emphasizes the faithfulness and trust of the lovers. The imagery also describes the nature of their love. The brooks are beautiful, and the fish stare at them, perhaps out of envy. The rivers are full of eels (life?) and the oceans have lovely sailing whales in them, which gives us the feeling of a floating quality, as if the lovers are locked in a world of romance.

5. In this love lyric, Leonard Cohen presents a vivid account of the feelings of a lover for his mistress. He seems to feel obliged to reassure her, and perhaps himself, of his faithfulness. We sense this is the ambiguous verb, "go"–if you go, or I command you to go; and in the increasing challenges he sets for their love, implied in brooks-rivers-oceans, and in "pass," "be long," and "not fail." He seems to be daring the fates to test his love. The intensity of his feelings is also suggested by the imagery and rhythm. In the brooks the fish stare quietly, in the rivers the eels "throng," and on the ocean the whales "sail." We feel the increase in passion here, from the idyllic love by a beautiful brook to the passion suggested by the thronging eels, to the power, beauty, and freedom of the sailing whales. The rhythm underlies this feeling because of the caesura in lines seven and eleven, and with the heavier spondaic rhythm of the last line, "I will not fail." Even the sounds seem to open and rise, from *brooks* to *rivers* to *oceans*. Overall this is a subtle poem about a brave young lover and the depth of his love.

If all student responses were as clearly delineated as these, then there would be little difficulty in defining levels of response. Nevertheless, by at least attempting to clarify for ourselves and more importantly for our students a consistent hierarchy of response, we can begin to teach and to evaluate. What do the responses above indicate?

Example No. 1 is the lowest level of response (excepting completely irrelevant ones, or no response at all). It indicates a superficial reading of the poem as a poem. There is evidence of some emotional reaction, but it is given in vague terms: "love-poem," "dreaminess," "romantic." The analogy to climbing mountains is perhaps close to the lover's feeling of bravado, but it is not elaborated beyond stock-response. Also, this student's perception is marred by his inclination to bring his own analogous experience to the poem *before* he has "read" the poem's experience properly. Analogy can often be a useful way for the student, who lacks critical terminology, to explain his reactions to a poem. In this case, however, the analogy to folk music does not clarify; it merely obscures. If this student could be led to describe a specific song which was *very* close to the poem's meaning, it might prove a profitable way of drawing the student nearer to the poem. Moreover, this student suffers from the fallacy that his own *opinion* (as opposed to his critical response) is of immense value. It is not, and this point must be made clear to him immediately.

We will call this kind of reaction the *Level of Stock-Response*. Its typical characteristics are: (1) generalized emotion usually predetermined in some way, (2) superficial reference to the elements of the poem, and (3) a confusion of personal opinion with genuine critical response.

Stock-Response is the lowest level simply because the student refuses to consider the poem as artefact; in fact, he usually brings preformed feelings and attitudes to it which make it impossible for him to read poetry seriously. In example No. 2 the problem is not dissimilar, except that here the student does read some details of the poem, but decides to make of them what he will. His response is almost as predictable as student No. 1, in that he is bound to generalize about the poem in the wildest fashion. These generalizations are not usually in the area of emotional response at all, but habitually take the form of unsubstantiated allegorizing or thematicizing. He is as far away from reading a poem as a complex pattern of idea and feeling as the stock-responder; his only advantage over the latter is that he does tend to examine some of the details of the poem and attempts to develop a consistent theory of what the poem might "mean."

We will call this type the *Level of Unsubstantiated Allegorical Response*. Its typical features are: (1) a tendency to describe themes or allegories in an elaborate manner, (2) a reticence to deal with obvious literal details, and (3) little or no attention to emotive or formal qualities of the poem.

Example No. 3 may not seem, at first glance, to be much superior to the first two, and in some ways is not. However, this student is closer to achieving a critical response than either the stock-responder or the allegorizer. For there is a steady focus on the poem itself, uncluttered by personal opinion, analogical exposition, or premature allegorizing. He has avoided stock-response by attempting to describe in more concrete terms the nature of the love involved: "telling her that he would be with her," "a beautiful place," "they plan to travel across oceans." There is evidence here that some connotative meaning has come through, that the student has a general idea of the situation in the poem (a lover talking about his love with his mistress) and that he has looked at some of the poem's details: "brooks," "rivers," "oceans," "I will not fail." However, there is little indication that he has got much beyond the literal meaning of such details, and when he has, his response to connotation is weak and partial. Note also that his attempt to comment directly on the emotion is given in general terms: "intense" and "very much in love."

We will call this kind of reaction the *Level of Literal Response*. Its typical characteristics are: (1) attention to specific details from the poem, (2) a literal recounting of these details, in some coherent fashion, with little or no connotative transfer, and (3) a generalized account (if any) of the poem's feeling: this may be accurate, though general, and thus is not really a stock-response. I would scale the Literal Response above the Stock-Response and the Unsubstantiated Allegorical Response, because it indicates that the student is at least looking at the poem. On the other hand, the student who writes a Stock- or Allegorical Response may be temperamentally more amenable to poetry as a medium once he has learned to examine it with some care. In fact, he may be "turned on" to poetry more quickly than the persistent literalist who can rarely pull his mind or imagination beyond the comfortable boundaries of the denotative. Nevertheless, the Literal Level is a necessary and prerequisite step for both the student with his stock-emotions and the one with his rarefied allegories. Unless each of them accedes to looking at the poem as artefact, neither can hope to attain a satisfactory response to poetry.

Example No. 4 is the kind of response which we hope would be typical of a large section of any English class. It reveals a sensitivity to the emotive details of the poem ("brooks are beautiful," "fish stare at them, perhaps out of envy") and also to individual structural features of the poem ("voice of the lover"–he has not automatically assumed that the speaker is the author, "she is far away"–he senses the dramatic situation in the poem, and he seems aware of the cumulative effect of the stanzas). Moreover, he is able to generalize accurately about the overall effect of images and statements within the poem: "he is reassuring her," "a floating quality," *etc.*

We will call this type the *Level of Connotative Response*. Its typical features are: (1) an accurate response to individual elements in the poem–images, sounds, rhetorical statements, rhythm, *etc.,* and (2) valid generalization from internal evidence, colored by a sensitivity to connotation. This level obviously goes beyond a literal reading, and avoids the pitfalls of premature allegorizing, predetermined emotional response, and amorphous subjectivity. It is not the highest level of response, but it is a valid one, a necessary step which all students of poetry must take.

Example No. 5 represents the highest level of response which we can reasonably expect from high school students. It reveals all the attributes of the Connotative Level, but adds to these a sense of completeness, a deeper response to the poem as a whole. This student has felt the patterns within the artefact–the expanding emotion indicated by the increasing intensity of the statements, the "growth" of the central water image (brooks–rivers–oceans), the shifts in rhythm and sound structure which reinforce this intensity. And he has been able to integrate the pattern into a *felt* response. (The literalist, it should be noted here, may be able to recount structural or rhetorical features but is unable to "read" their meaning any better than he is imagery or metaphor.)

We will call this type the *Level of Pattern-Response*. Its typical characteristics are: (1) a deep and integrated response to the connotations of image, symbol, sound structure, logic and/or rhetoric, *etc.*, (2) a sense of these verbal patterns giving shape to a whole experience, and (3) an awareness of the integration of the emotive and cognitive aspects of poetry. Of course, few students will respond fully to all of the patterns or all of the separate images and structural signals in a poem, but the attempt to come to grips with these will be present and at least partially realized. Of course, there are other levels of response beyond Pattern-Response, and individual gifted youngsters may achieve these; for example, the mythological level, or the allusive (Cohen's poem has overtones of both, with its Biblical effects in sound and image, its use of water as a controlling symbol). However, our central concern in the high schools is to bring *all* students up to the Connotative Level, and as many as possible to the level of Pattern-Response.

Two disclaimers must be made here. First, these five levels of response are in no way psychologically valid categories of thought or feeling (in the sense that Bloom's taxonomy is); they are merely rhetorical categories which are essentially descriptive, and thus verifiable only in context and in operation. Second, they do not represent all the possible kinds of responses which students might derive from a poem. Any practicing teacher will recognize that student responses do not appear in such a clear and defining light as the hypothetical examples I have used. Nevertheless, these five levels represent basic and repeated *kinds* of responses, and as such can provide teacher and student with a hierarchy of responses, a general framework within which literary growth can be nourished, examined, and evaluated.

For example, the teacher could use this hierarchy initially as a diagnostic tool. The wild allegorizer must be shown why his responses are invalid in a literary sense, and this means that his teacher must learn to recognize this tendency early, describe it to him in specific terms, and show him by reference to the higher levels achieved by others in the class just where he has to go. The stock-responder must learn to read literally and then connotatively and then in a patterned way. It is only through a precise *description* of these levels and their hierarchical nature that the student can assess his *own* growth. Diagnosis of basic responsive problems thus becomes possible; it is then up to the teacher to go beyond the diagnosis and develop teaching strategies which will foster such growth.

Finally, a rough system of evaluation becomes possible as an ultimate test of what the student has learned about the process of reading, and what success the teacher himself has had in challenging his class to reach beyond their present level of understanding.

When diagnosis and evaluation become possible, so do teaching strategies. Lessons can be designed to combat the grosser results of Wimsatt's Affective Fallacy: stock response, subjective opinionizing, unsubstantiated generalization. And when these have been resolved by attention to the Literal and Connotative Levels, work can begin on the deeper and more rewarding level of Pattern-Response. The main pedagogical point to be emphasized here is that these levels are successive and interdependent.

Finally, any rhetorical or pedagogical structure can only be operable within the larger context of teaching literature–a context shaped by the kind of clear definitional framework outlined in Part One: where the nature of poetry and how it means, its complicated hybrid forms, its proper place in the contemporary complex of ideas and experience can be examined in a classroom atmosphere which is conducive to real learning, untrammeled by elitism, moralizing, and hypocritical postures.

Literature, as Wimsatt implies, is too important to be taught badly–or carelessly.

Foot Notes:
[1] W. K. Wimsatt, Jr., "The Affective Fallacy" in *The Verbal Icon* (Lexington: University of Kentucky Press, 1967, p. 38. All succeeding quotations from Wimsatt have been taken from *The Verbal Icon* and page numbers refer to this text.
[2] Northrop Frye, *The Educated Imagination.* Toronto: C.B.C. Publications, 1963, p. 36.
[3] From *Selected Poems: 1956-1968* by Leonard Cohen. Copyright in all countries of the International Copyright Union. All rights reserved. Reprinted by permission of The Viking Press.

– 08 –

The Subject-Centred Curriculum:
Last Chance or Lost Cause?

English Quarterly, vol. 4, no. 4 (Fall, 1971)

I

As an incurable believer in lost causes, I wish to argue in favour of a subject-centred school curriculum. Since my areas of competence are English and the school system of Ontario, they will form the basis for my argumentation, though I suspect that what I have to say will have broader implications. The timing of this paper may seem curiously anachronistic, yet it is precisely because of three recent developments in education that I feel we need a thorough reexamination of some of our basic premises and not a few of our assumptions and prejudices. Two of these developments are "new" and one of them is "old" (but still very much with us): the child-centred/activities-oriented curriculum, the behavioral objectives movement, and the so-called (ancient) subject curriculum. The first two are really current reactions to the old model, and must be examined in this light.

The passion for child-centred education revolving around an activities-model is best exemplified by the Hall-Dennis Report,[1] which presents a frontal assault on the "out moded" subject curriculum, and in its place would have a school where the child's needs would be paramount, dictating the activities and determining the strategies of the teacher, subordinating subject-interest to personal-interest, and demanding a psychological rather than a disciplinary model for the curriculum. Affect over cognition, personal growth over intellectual attainment. *Living and Learning*, if nothing else, is a stimulating dialectical document.[2] Its influence can be seen in a cursory reading of a recent Ontario Department of Education curriculum guideline for "English" in grades seven to ten, from which these arresting sentences have been taken: "Today there is a keen awareness that human beings learn through activity and retain best what they have come to understand through their own initiative," or "The purpose of these guidelines is to assist teachers to broaden their concept of English as a vehicle of learning. The point at issue is not 'What is English?' The question instead is 'Which learning situations will best develop the receptive and the expressive abilities of students as individuals?'" or "Thus, in the Intermediate Division [grades 7-10], English can no longer be treated as a subject for study."[3] The attack on English as a subject or discipline is more than implicit. Furthermore, this attack is not by any means limited to Ontario or Hall-Dennis. John Dixon's book, *Growth Through* English,[4] a summary of the landmark Dartmouth Seminar of 1966, offers a compelling argument for a personal growth theory, and is indicative of a larger movement sweeping Great Britain. In Canada, even at the high school level, where subject-disciplines have been holding their own, the trend toward electives in English—film, drama, journalism, Canadian studies, and various sociological theme units—is an ominous sign of things to come. A tide has been loosed, somewhere, and we are caught up in it.

I am not implying here that I disagree *in toto* with many of the sentiments of this movement, nor am I about to offer a detailed criticism of *Living and Learning* and its analogues (others have done this better than I could).[5] I would like merely to point out the dangers inherent in the child-centred/activities approach. Without question, English as a subject is adrift, and the implications of this drift must be studied with some care and purpose. In general terms, for example, a curriculum model defined only by activities (looking at books, watching films, composing a class newspaper, *etc.*) and free from intellectual controls of *any* kind will result in incidental learning only, which may or may not be recognized and reinforced. Without a rational, guiding framework which would include an intellectual structure and a coherent pedagogy in addition to personal and social (*i.e.* educational) aims, both teacher and pupil are adrift. More important, both are left open to the unwarranted social pressures of a society which is increasingly permissive, sectarian, and pragmatic. The result could be a classroom where the teacher is intimidated by his pupils' demands for "relevance" and the parents' demands for some kind of accountability, with no guarantee that anything has been learned. This is not to say that literary activities are not an important pedagogical instrument. They are. And therein lies the seductive attraction of the new theories. But activities are the manifestation of certain cognitive and affective models—in whole or in part, completed or becoming. They imply shape and purpose; they are indices of growth when set against a wider screen of knowledge and understanding, and thus become in the hands of an intelligent teacher powerful tools for motivation, reinforcement, and measurement. In brief, activities are the concrete operations through which the child begins to discern the structure of his world, inside and out, and learns to understand and manipulate it. The danger, then, of a naïve activities approach and a pseudo-sentimental focus on the child's "needs" is that activities themselves are likely to be divorced from the cognitive and affective matrix of which they are an integral part, with a resultant confusion in educational aims and procedures, and potentially disastrous effects on learning of any kind.

It is precisely this sort of confusion which the behavioral objectives proponents feed upon. Although this movement has not yet affected Canada to any extent, it is already a powerful force in American education. With funding from the U.S. Office of Education a committee composed of twenty-eight of the best-known English teachers, professors, and educators has embarked on a two-year project entitled *A Catalog of Behavioral Objectives for English in Grades 9 to 12.* This study could well be prototype and blueprint for

English teachers everywhere in America's high schools. The dangers and "advantages" of this approach to learning and teaching are clearly spelled out in a recent NCTE publication *On Writing Behavioral Objectives for English*; Canadian teachers would do well to read it in advance of the event. In general, it is a systems analysis approach involving the detailed specification of objectives in terms which make them amenable to empirical or "objective" verification. In this way not only can learning be measured accurately (they say) but the teacher's performance as well, so that he can be made specifically *accountable* for all his actions. Moreover, new curriculum programs can be assessed, and either promoted or dismissed. It is an accountant's Utopia, a trustee's dream of Eden realized, for now everyone–the public, administrators, teachers, and students–will know exactly what has "transgressed" in the classroom; reward and punishment can be dispensed with Puritan simplicity and computer-like charity.

It is the accountability factor of this approach which is hopelessly enticing to a public weary of high education costs, baffled by the unsubstantiated claims of left-wing reform-groups, and genuinely confused by school curricula which appear to have no clear rationale. These three conditions are becoming more and more a feature of education in Canada as we dutifully ape the actions of our southern cousins (with a respectable ten-year time-lag), and one of the few certainties in a rather unpredictable future will be the "discovery" by our own boards of education of the behavioralist panacea. And the more we ourselves are confused about the curricula we are producing, the greater the danger that systems analysis will "have" to be instituted as the final solution.

One does not have to spell out in detail the effects of behavioral objectives on programs in the humanities,[6] but one of the ironies of this approach must be immediately recognized: it appears to restore the subject to the centre of the curriculum while essentially emasculating it. English, and History and French and Classics will be subjects in a *topical* sense only; their radical disciplinary foundations–hierarchical concept-building, sequence in activity and formulation, synthesis and integration, psychological and social contextuality, and, most significant, the genuine open-ended exploration of experience with its unmeasurable randomness and chance intuition–all this will disappear in the specification of multiple objectives and the ruthless testing of observable behaviors.[7] Nevertheless, it is more than likely that parents will be pleased to know what little Susie is "learning," trustees will be happy with an infallible accounting system, pupils will have a new and easier game to play, and teachers will learn, reluctantly, to join in the fun.

We have been looking, then, at the two possible extremes in future curriculum theory and design–a sort of chaos or accountability equation with a negative equal-sign, both of which are presented as drastic solutions to what has preceded them–that is, the curricula and teaching methods of the 1950's and 1960's. Hall-Dennis has attached these as sterile and discipline-centred. The behavioralists will see them (*and* Hall-Dennis) as disorganized and uneducational. Both assaults, it is my contention, are based on a serious misreading of the "old" curriculum. They are, at best, solutions to the wrong problem.

What, then, was (is) the "old way"? First, the curriculum (certainly in the elementary schools of Ontario) is not and has never been subject-centred. "Reading", spelling, punctuation, memory work, penmanship, "grammar" rules, *etc.* are not the discipline of language and literature, no matter how many ways they may be shuffled. They are skills and/or activities associated with and necessary to an understanding of language and literature. But if the teacher is unaware (as so many were and are) of their relationship to the very discipline of which they are part, then they remain isolated skills or topics. Similarly, a content-centred social studies course is not yet, nor may not become, a social science: classroom chat about Canadian "history" is likely to be something other than history[8]; (Mathematics and Science have fared better, having been recently reorganized along lines suggested by Jerome Bruner[9]). A true subject-centred curriculum is one based on the relevant discipline at the highest and broadest levels. In English, this discipline is practised daily by scholars, critics, teachers, book reviewers, writers, readers, and "responders" in general. As Bruner points out, teaching a discipline at various levels of education is essentially a problem in finding ways of making the questions, procedures, and concepts of that discipline understandable, accessible, and meaningful to a student in a context which involves both his individual and social world-view. (More on this later).

Seen in this light, a disciplinary teaching has not been systematically carried out in the elementary schools of Ontario. How many of our children, for example, realize the interrelatedness of such skills as reading, writing, listening, talking, viewing, and performing? Or the fundamental rhetorical similarity of novel reading and letter writing? How many see English, even dimly, as personally meaningful, a *way* of viewing the world and discovering themselves through the discipline of language? How many realize that the *kind* of thinking-activities even in English class is distinctly different from that of Science or History? These are more than rhetorical questions.

The high schools of Ontario have fared better, but given the more clearly delineated subject-curriculum, specialist-trained teachers, and students moving into a more abstract stage of thinking, they should have been able to do much more than they have done thus far. Again, I would suggest that their subject too often has been topically defined, and has suffered from the same abuses as those found in the elementary school–an emphasis on skills and compartmentalized learning–and some new ones of their own devising: premature scholasticism and esthetics, a separating of the cognitive from the affective (especially in testing), and in general, a failure to see the essential disciplinary unity underlying the diverse elements of the subject. As a result, the real meaning (and effect) of form is lost; the problems of belief and verification, which lie at the heart of literary study, are ignored; and most important, the moral dimension inherent in language, rhetoric, and literature is not felt by students, or, what is worse, is reduced to subjective moralizing or an unstructured discussion of "values".[10]

What I am saying here is that the child-centred/activities approach, which was suddenly and arbitrarily introduced into Ontario, was a reaction, and to some extent a legitimate one, against the practices of a decade, but one which was based on a serious misreading of these practices. Since no real disciplinary approach was attempted in elementary school, and only a fitful one in high school, this new method could not be an antidote for the so-called disciplinary one. What it is replacing is the confused and ill-conceived attempt to teach "subjects", using poorly trained personnel (mostly teachers with summer school or short-course types of teacher-training). The activities approach may indeed be better than its predecessor, since even incompetent teachers can be programmed to initiate activities, and much incidental learning may occur, and at the least, student attitudes to the materials and activities may be changed for the better.

In deciding on a panacea for the problems of the sixties, however, those in positions of authority ignored an alternative solution: a genuine subject-centred curriculum of the kind outlined above. It cannot be emphasized too much that this alternative was not considered because it was assumed that it had already been tried—and had fallen short. Neither conclusion is valid. It has *never* seriously been tried in elementary school, while in high school it has been proven successful by an unnoticed but sizable minority of teachers.

If and when the behavioral objectives arrive on the scene, we should point out to them that *their* panacea has already been tried. For what has been going on for ten years (or more) at both levels has been a form of objectivist teaching, albeit unwittingly. The obsession with measurable units has plagued English teaching, and other subject areas, for decades. The grammarian in grade six who fits all pupils to the same parsable measuring stick, the grade eight teacher who "drills" topic sentences as if they were Platonic absolutes, the high school teacher who demands a uniform interpretation for the weekly sonnet—all are equally addicted to quantitative measurement. And thus, a full-blown behavioral objectives *system* will only compound the problems in our schools, in spite of any inherent value it may or may not have. It would reinforce the prejudices and practices of the many undisciplinary teachers, bewilder recent converts to the activities approach, and inhibit those teachers presently groping their way towards a reasoned and reasonable disciplinary model. (A fourth model, of course, and one promulgated by Hall-Dennis enthusiasts, is the interdisciplinary one—an offshoot of the child-centred/activities model. This makes some sense at levels one to six, where the child has no intellectual grasp of disciplines or categories of thought-feelings; but it follows from this that learning activities at this stage are merely non-disciplinary, or more accurately, *pre*disciplinary. True interdisciplinary activity takes place at the *highest* levels of man's thinking; and moreover, it has always occurred, and is still occurring—modern "pedagogicalists" did not discover it. For example, Marshall McLuhan evolved into a media-magician through the unmagical realms of literary criticism; Northrop Frye has nicely combined theology and mythology; and behavioralists like Bruner and Jackson have come some way from the little-red-Skinner-houses which bred them. However, between grade six and graduate school, neither a non-disciplinary nor an interdisciplinary approach seems reasonable nor desirable.[11])

To sum up this part: in order to overcome our obvious failure to teach children very much despite massive public investment in the schools, we have begun to introduce curriculum models which are child-centred/activities-oriented, which find their sanction in a permissive and uninformed public and a general demand for relevance, and appear on the surface to be a reaction against the so-called subject-centred curriculum. Behind both models lies the spectre of the behavioral scientist—the mountebank with the pill to end all pills.

II

It is probably already too late to reverse the trend toward the non-disciplinary curriculum, in English studies at least. Or perhaps there is a last chance, for this decade. Either way, I wish to advocate a genuine disciplinary model that will not only clarify an otherwise confused curriculum, but will also provide a centre from which the teacher can meet the challenges of relevance and individualization, and make the grosser elements of behavioralist specification unnecessary and redundant. In this brief space I can only indicate the broad outlines of a complex theory and suggest some background readings.

We begin with Bruner's thesis that "any subject can be taught effectively in some intellectually honest form to any child at any stage of development",[12] and take it seriously. Whether or not all elements of his proposition hold true can be seen only when English scholars and critics and teachers have thought about them honestly and attempted to translate them into curricular ideas, pedagogical strategies, and classroom learning situations. At the moment, in Ontario, we have dismissed the thesis,[13] and opted for models whose theoretical basis is shaky to say the least. On the other hand, English as a discipline has been and is continuing to be defined for us by critics, linguists, writers, and teachers at all levels.[14] The material is available, and what is surprising, when one reads through it, is not the numerous differences of opinion but the degree of consensus–and this in spite of the various starting points and scholarly hobby-horsing. One begins to see–in outline form–that linguistics, rhetoric, and literature are fully compatible with such educational objectives as personal growth, individual development, open-ended instruction, discovery techniques, *etc*. Indeed, at certain levels and for certain groups of students, curricula and pedagogical strategies are presently being worked out with some hope of success.[15]

One theme common to much of this literature is that English involves a way of looking at the world, of ordering reality, of defining a sense of self; it implies a certain kind of validity (or proof) and entails specific problems of belief and applicability to life;[16] it has moral as well as esthetic value. And running like a contrapuntal motif through all of this is the equally pervasive idea that language as a symbolizing process makes specific demands of those–at any age–who come to use it: demands of form, of context, of denotative and connotative reference, of time and place; and that fundamental *language -forms* (*e.g.*, noun/verb symbols, sentence transformations, generative metaphor) are the model for the *rhetorical forms* they make possible (story, poem, dialogue, paragraph, periodicity, simile, rhythm, *etc*.); *i.e.* each make similar kinds of demands on the user, each functions as an organizing as well as a limiting device upon experience, and each is, in its own manner, a kind of formal "reality", something outside us which we transform within prescribed limits however infinite they may seem, and which we "make our own." Literature is seen, then, as an extension of the basic language/rhetoric model, sharing with it the demands made by form and symbol-reading, and enriching it through an amazingly sophisticated use of rhetoric, metaphor, and the rhythmic potentialities of the sentence-function. The genres and modes, created over thousands of years out of man's need for literary expression and experience, are merely more abstract and meaning-laden forms of the fundamental symbolization process that was implicit in our first spoken word.[17] Man, of course, developed parallel means to symbolize, know, and control his world: painting, architecture, music, clothing, and more recently the moving picture in film and television.[18] Literary modes have influenced these and in turn have been influenced by them. Thus, a disciplinary approach to English does not exclude drama or film or T.V.–it subsumes them. Similarly, the social uses of language, for good or evil (propaganda, advertising, journalism, jargons, *etc.*) are extensions of the original potential in all language.

What all this means, in simple terms, is that when we teach English (whether it be creative drama, *Wuthering Heights*, "Midnight Cowboy" or "Ode to a Nightingale"), we are teaching, obliquely or directly, the discipline of language, which happens to be, in this case, our own. The general statements made above about language, rhetoric, and literature can, I think, be agreed upon by most teachers. In a very general sense, then, it is true to say that we do have a subject. Our areas of disagreement, on the other hand, would include the following: 1) the way in which individuals come to learn language best (though much work has been done on this); 2) the pace at and degree to which pupils can absorb the successively abstractive demands of language; 3) the problem of defining the absolute and relative dimensions of words, sentences, literary artefacts, *etc.*; 4) the various critical approaches to literature, each claiming possession of the sacred ground; 5) the extent to which language study can be defended on utilitarian grounds (*i.e.* its social benefits). There are, no doubt, others. And doubtless the major difficulty in presenting English as a discipline to students (and teachers) is the apparent disagreement about its "fundamental" concepts. I am suggesting that a careful reading of the recent literature on English will reveal major areas of consensus. It will also reassure the humanist heart beating in the breast of every English teacher that English is indeed a humanity, an open-ended exploration of experience through the potentialities of language, so complex and brilliant an achievement that we are impatient because we can sense, feel, and manipulate its power (as a child can) and yet are unable fully to categorize it or control its growth within us. But that is not to say that language is therefore not comprehendible, that it will not submit to the scrutiny of our categorizing rationality, that we cannot learn enough about it to build a pedagogical framework within which to teach it to those who rightfully deserve something better than relevant activities or preformulated behavioral objectives.

We have a subject, then; a discipline. We are, here and there, on the verge of discovering how to teach it in an "intellectually honest way" to our young people. What we need most is time, and less panic. And no more panaceas. The disciplinary English curriculum will not provide us with quick results. But any results achieved will be valid ones. What alternatives do we really have? An activities model, on the one hand, with its shapeless busy-work and pandering to student "needs," and on the other hand, a behavioralist model (implied or explicit) with its simple credos and stultifying procedures. Both can be avoided when the discipline itself gives shape, direction, and meaning to a course of study. From such a theoretical base, all forms of linguistic, rhetorical and literary *activity* can take place to suit the real learning needs of individual students. Nothing is out of place if it ultimately has a place. And only a teacher thoroughly steeped in the certainties (and the insecurities) of his subject can foster growth in and through language.

But where lie the keys to this dreamland? The first one is to be found in our universities. Subject-competent teachers must first be trained where the discipline is most deeply felt and revered. Much soul-searching and some immediate action is necessary here, if one can judge by the kind of students entering the College of Education–lugging a satchel full of facts, prejudices, unintegrated chunks of literary thinking, and little or no linguistics. Second, teachers in elementary and high school must be retrained, not only in pedagogical methods but in their basic approach to language and literature. Finally, the major burden rests with the teaching-training institutions, who must produce a new breed of teacher, help with updating the profession, and bring more overt pressure to bear upon school boards and departments of education.

This is, obviously, no panacea. In the short term much could be achieved if each teacher took some time to read a little of the relevant literature, or in the least, reflected seriously about his own work. The long term may just take care of itself.

III

To take the matter one more step, and a foot deeper. The real problem in English (and other subjects) is not merely "bad teaching". In fact, there may be no cure for this disease, considering the state of human nature and the present condition of North American society. The crucial question in educating the young, especially in the humanities, is the one concerned with freedom and authority.[18] Much has been written recently about freedom in learning (Holt, Illyich, Friedenberg, *etc.*), but little about authority, except to depict is as a negative of freedom. The practical effect of this sustained assault on the so-called "system" may well be the annihilation of the present bureaucratic and hierarchical structure of education, and few of us would mourn for the victim. But if bureaucratic "authority," posing as representative of the social/political will, were to be destroyed, or seriously undermined (witness the recent financial cutbacks in Ontario, and the growing demands for accountability and reassessment), what new structure would replace it? At present our options would include: Rousseauesque "free-schools", the Marxist/Maoist/Leninist educational emporium, the Freudian non-school, the utilitarian degree factory controlled by systems analysis, or, more likely in Canada, a community-oriented school where political, social, and in-group pressures would predominate. None of these options, it seems to me, offer the child either freedom or education. Each of them places authority in the hands of a new power-élite, with no guarantee that their particular brand will be any better than the one they have replaced.

In discussing freedom in education, we should keep in mind what Northrop Frye has said about the subject in *The Educated Imagination*:

You see, *freedom has nothing to do with lack of training; it can only be the product of training.* You're not free to move unless you've learned to walk, and not free to play the piano unless you practice. Nobody is capable of free speech unless he knows how to use the language, and such knowledge is not a gift: it has to be learned and worked at. [Italics mine] (p. 64)

He is arguing, of course, for an education of the imagination grounded in the discipline of language and literature, from which it obtains its authority. The first thing our imaginations have to do for us, as soon as we can handle words well enough to read and write and talk, *is to fight to protect us from falling into the illusions that society threatens us with.* [Italics mine] (p. 60) Some of these "illusions" are to be found in what passes for the educational theory of our time.

What Frye is suggesting, and what has been implicit in this paper throughout, is an education dedicated to freeing our children by putting into their hands (and heads) the *means* by which they can define, describe, imagine, and act upon their world. This involves the slow and onerous task of coming to understand and control the *categories* of thought and feeling which Western Man throughout his history has sought to discover, define, and re-define. These are the disciplines inherent in the arts and sciences. Despite the present attacks on them (some of them justified in part but not in whole), these disciplines continue to grow, both horizontally and vertically. They have been subject to all the customary failings of the humans exploring them, but this is no reason to dismiss them as rigid, stultifying, class-oriented, discriminative, fascistic, *et al.* Some of us may be guilty of making the discipline of English fit these labels, here and there, and from time to time. But the growth of the imagination is still our best educational goal. And the means of achieving it have not changed radically: words, metaphors, visual and musical forms, mathematical symbolism, empirical experimentation. They breathe life into the human spirit, and through them each of us finds the way to the only kind of freedom possible: the freedom to know and to choose.

Ultimately, then, one is never debating about preferred systems, pedagogies, or curricula. These will come and go, as intellectual or social fashion dictates. Rather, we are being confronted with a challenge which involves the kind of authority to which our children will be subjected in the 1970's: that is, which special-interest group will wreak its will on us? Teachers and professional educators, the current jargon asserts, have had their chance, and failed. No doubt we have. But the experiment in *mass education* is less than ten years old in Canada. New ways of developing a truly meaningful discipline-centred course in English (and other subjects) are just now being explored. We need time. And commitment from our classroom teachers. And much clear thinking about the essential issues—free from jargon, fashion, personal whim, and outside pressures.

In brief, I am making a special plea for those teachers whose goals are directed towards the growth of imagination to hang on, to resist the tides sweeping over them. At the same, time, they must breathe new life into their methods and procedures, adapt to change where necessary, but never lose sight of the worthwhile goals implicit in a discipline-centred form of education.

After all, English teachers have always specialized in lost causes.

References:

[1] *Living and Learning,* Ontario Department of Education (Toronto, 1968).

[2] For a detailed and learned critique of *Living and Learning,* see Brian Crittenden, ed., *Means and Ends,* O.I.S.E. (Toronto, 1969).

For a discussion of polarization in educational thinking, see also J. M. Paton, "The Either/Or Syndrome in Education Theorizing," *Teacher Education* (Spring 1969).

[3] Ontario Department of Education, *English: Intermediate Division* (Toronto, 1969), p. 3.

[4] John Dixon, *Growth Through English,* N.A.T.E. (Reading, 1967).

[5] See note (2). Of especial significance is Crittenden's discussion of the child's needs in his essay "Means and Ends."

[6] See the papers by Summerfield, Moffett and Hogan in John Maxwell and Anthony Tovatt, eds., *On Writing Behavioral Objectives in English,* N.C.T.E. (Champaign, I11., 1970).

[7] For example in a recent behavioral objectives pilot-project in California, we find the description of *several hundred* objectives for a grade eight English class—each one requiring one or more "tests."

[8] See A. B. Hodgetts, *What Culture? What Heritage?* O.I.S. E. (Toronto, 1968).

[9] See Jerome Bruner, *The Process of Education* (Cambridge, Mass., 1960), and *Towards a Theory of Instruction* (Cambridge, Mass., 1966), chapters 1, 3, and 5. Also, Prof. Paul Park has been working at Althouse College of Education and O.I.S.E. to develop an environmental approach to science, based on his experience with Nuffield Project. Here, an exciting new methodology has been wedded to the teaching of basic scientific principles and concepts to young children.

[10] For an analysis of the moral dimension in language and literature, see William Walsh, *The Use of Imagination* (London, 1959), particularly chapters 8 and 10.

[11] Inter(anti?)-disciplinary enthusiasts seem to ignore much of the work that has been done on the rhythm of education by Piaget and Bruner. Whitehead's "ancient" book *The Aims of Education* is still relevant reading. Even James Britton, an advocate of the personal growth theory, said at the Dartmouth Seminar: "Our aim, then should be to refine and develop responses the children are already making . . . . Development can best be described as an increasing sense of form."   (*Response to Literature,* N.C.T.E., 1968, p. 4). Form is an essential element of the discipline of English, and Britton is arguing, implicitly, a case for the disciplinary approach.

[12] Jerome Bruner, *The Process of Education* (Cambridge, 1960), p. 33.

[13] See particularly, John Stevens, "My Occupation—A Mystery?" *Teacher Education* (Spring 1969), pp. 16-24, and my reply, Don Gutteridge, "Teaching Structure in English," *English Quarterly,* III, 2 (Summer 1970), pp. 38-49.

[14] Frye, Leavis, Wimsatt, Walsh (critics), Booth, Chomsky, Halliday, Gleason, Joos (linguists—rhetoricians), Britton, Dixon, Moffett, Squire (pedagogues)—to name just a few in each category.

[15] For example, the Pilot Project in Mass Media developed by the Ontario Department of Education for non-academic high school classes: *the Language in Use* curriculum developed by linguists, scholars, and teachers through the British Schools Council. Also O.I.S.E. has published *Rhetoric: A Unified Approach to English Curricula* (Toronto, 1970), which presents teachers with a unifying subject-theory and dozens of practical teaching units. See also, James Moffett, *A Student-Centred Language Arts Curriculum, Grades K-13* (Boston, 1968).

[16] See Northrop Frye, *The Well-Tempered Critic* (Indiana, 1963): chapter three is a clearly reasoned essay on the nature and purpose of literature.

[17] A good introduction to language as symbol may be found in Susanne K. Langer, *Philosophy in a New Key* (New York, 1951), chapter 1 -5.

[18] The keynote address by James R. Squire to the *York Conference: Teaching and Learning English,* 1971, was entitled "Freedom and Control, the Scylla and Charybdis of Language Learning."

– 09 –

Teaching the Canadian Mythology:
A Poet's View

After ten years of writing poems, mainly on Canadian historical subjects, I have discovered that, like all serious poets, I had been a maker of myths. This should have come as no surprise to me, and yet it did. Perhaps I was just too busy writing the poems to worry about such larger critical and affective aspects of the literature to which I was annually contributing. But events in this country during the past five years have compelled me (and many others) to think more carefully about the significance of our literature in relation to Canada as an emergent "nation."

Myth, of course, is an elusive word, one that has been used, willy-nilly, to bolster the arguments and underpin the hypotheses of critics, psychologists, sociologists, historians, poly-sci enthusiasts, ad-men, and politicians of every blush and hue–each in his own way, perhaps, questing for the golden key to our lost identity. In fact, this quest has become the national pastime, the Canadian quiz-game with myth as the secret word. I have no intention of reviewing or commenting upon the many-splendored meanings of myth nor the dreary uses to which they have been put. I wish merely to define, as precisely as I can, the way in which myth operates for me as a poet, and mention some of the significant ways in which, I feel, it bears upon the question of our identity, both personal and public.

One "myth" (to use the word in its most common and least fortunate sense) which should be swept aside at the outset is the mistaken notion that we have no identity, or at best a very nebulous one, and therefore, instead of discovering it or bringing it to the consciousness, we must somehow *create* one–and fast, before the nasty Americans or the upstart Quebecois overwhelm us with their own clearly delineated cultures. It is this silly notion which has diluted our collective energies and distorted our national goals for the past two decades. To put the record straight, and quite simply, we *have* an identity because we *are*, and *have been*. We are and have been occupying this space called Canada for three centuries; for over a hundred years we have referred to ourselves as a nation, and have, more or less, behaved as if we were one. What kind of nation, what sort of people, what forms underlying our national purpose, our common pursuits, our destiny–these are legitimate questions, even yet, one hundred and four years after the official natal rites. However, as I suggested, this country, at least its English speaking portion (and I suspect, despite the ruder noises, the French-speaking section as well)–this country seems gripped with an anxiety approaching hysteria and manifesting not a little paranoid-schizophrenia, a blind and self-defeating fear that maybe, after all, we don't exist. Our mirror is a window. Well, it just isn't so. We have existed, and we do.

To argue this point fully would require a separate (and longer) paper, but let me just mention several pertinent points at this stage. Northrop Frye has noted that this kind of anxiety over identity leads to the creation of a social mythology. And much of our identity-hunting in Canada has been of this variety—with all its inherent dangers: self-delusion, commercialization, and ultimate loss of true identity. For our true identity can only be realized, as it has been in each of us as individuals, by questing within, not without, by moving below the surface patterns of our everyday life to that area just beneath consciousness, where the forms of our feeling are known to lie, and where we can apprehend them, free from the pressures and the mirages of the chaos above. This is precisely what the adolescent, what each individual who seeks to be uniquely human, must do. It has its dangers, no doubt, for both individual and group. But one of the dangers is *not* that we will find nothing. What we will find are the myths, the blueprints which have given and will continue to give our lives, separately or collectively, their unique *curve of meaning*. We may not like what we see, but it exists and is real enough.

The second point to be made here is that the arts, and literature in particular, have traditionally been the repository for myths, the myths of the individual writer fashioning his work of art and through it the myths of the society out of which and for whom he is writing. (I will elaborate on this further on.) In brief, the mark of a nation, or society, or civilization, as Kenneth Clark reminds us, is its culture, its myriad art-*forms*. Canadians have had a literature, of some kind, from the very beginning. This literature has steadily grown in magnitude and quality; and because it is literature, it does contain myths, which because of their peculiar nature will tell us what we were, where we thought we were going, what we are, and might become.

But how? What is myth in this restricted literary sense? In what way can it provide us with forms of identity? Northrop Frye has dealt extensively (and accurately, I feel) with literary myth in what I would call the critical or general sense. I would like to come at the problem from the inside, from the point of view of the poet who "makes" myths, in order to clarify some crucial points about their nature and the manner in which they operate in literary works.

For the poet, there are three areas of concern ("levels" if you will) in the making of a poem: 1) words and rhetorics, 2) symbols, and 3) myths. He begins with words, with what they can express, and what they can be made to do rhetorically. Rhythm and logic and grammar and sound and genre come into play. In a sense, the identity-game begins here. In the quest for words and their rhetorical patterns, the poet is seeking to define in himself what heretofore has been indefinable, or merely vague or shapeless or inchoate. But words, as rudimentary symbols, give back as much meaning as they give off. For the poet this is always a symbiotic process: the self and the language of the self, not identical but *identifying*. Rudimentary word-symbols, grammars, rhetorics—all move easily into the area of literary symbolism. There is no difference here in kind, only of intensity, focus, portability and the potential for interaction. A symbol is a cluster of minor "symbols" (metaphor, character, action, *etc.*), but more than the sum of its contributors. Consequently, it will say more–will give off more meaning and give back more than the poet expects. At both levels, word and symbol, the aim is to create a *rhetorical brilliance*, in which the penumbra carries the meaning out as well as in. In each instance, the poet is identifying in himself what has been only potential. And, of course, at this point, there are really no clearly marked "levels."

It must be stressed here, too, that this process is exploratory. In the best poems, the true poems, words and symbols have a way of "choosing" themselves. It is more accurate to say that meaning is found or discovered rather than created. Identifying, or knowing one's identity, is an act of discovery, of disclosure. The meaning is there: to be revealed, not promulgated.

I emphasize this point because when the poet moves toward myth the exploratory nature of his work is heightened, becomes infinitely more subtle and "mysterious" (*i.e.* less easily definable). Myth, in the poem, is the deepest shape of meaning, the point of closest identity between the self and its defining language. It can only be reached (revealed, discovered) through the other two layers or textures of the identifying process. Which is to say that the poet must find his words first, he must make *them* mean so deeply that they take on new configurations and become symbols for him, to be re-worked until they too are *brilliant* filigrees of meaning. At this point, if he is lucky enough and good enough, the myths will reveal themselves. For, in one sense, myth was the pattern that was there all along (or seemed so), that was influencing the choice of word and symbol, that was ordering the configurations underlying the rhetoric at both levels. Seen from another angle, it is the pattern created by and yet creating the complex of word and symbol. (Which comes first is a question much debated for centuries and, for the poet at least, not really relevant).

The general point I'm driving at here is that the poet cannot start with the myth. He does not choose it; he works toward it, and finds it. ("Bad" poets and "bad" poetry will probably not conform to the rule, but this is a separate, if no less interesting, problem). The reader of poems re-enacts the process, beginning with the surface rhetoric and working in and out, back and forth. Thus he is able to identify, through the language of identity, the myth and all its meaning. He is able to recognize a sense of self "other" than his own, and insofar as he is affected by the poem, may identify elements of his own self. If the poet belongs to the reader's own culture, or nation, the common elements of the symbol-patterns (the mythology of the poem) may be more numerous and recognizable than otherwise. Besides the universally human nature of the myths discovered, there will be a level of identification which can only be described as *nation-al*. For what is a nation but a collection of *othernesses*, some of whose elements are mutually felt and understood by its individual members?

Let me illustrate the foregoing by reference to some of my own recent work. I have to date written poems about Dollard, the Jesuits, Hudson, LaSalle, Champlain, Riel, and Hearne. These figures, for me, have served the function of symbols. They have been able, through the poems I have built around and out of them, to tell me things about myself. This is the prime motive for writing–the self-seeking of a language of identification. But I did not choose these personages in any literal sense. I have always read widely and erratically in Canadian history. Certain figures would hold my interest more than others. If this interest seemed inexplicable to me in ordinary terms, I would try writing a poem. There was something to be explained, discovered. Always I began with the poem, the words. I could tell after a few lines or one or two sittings whether or not the words had any *brilliance* to them. If they did not, I abandoned the work. Certain figures, despite several attempts, yielded nothing; *e.g.* Sir Guy Carleton, an adolescent idol of mine; or Brébeuf, whose place was eventually taken in my "Coureurs de Bois" by a fictional priest who seemed more compatible. Five years later, I was able to write a quite different poem about the great Jesuit ("Brébeuf on the Cross"). What I am saying is that the symbol cannot be chosen consciously, and that the serious and honest poet can determine the integrity of his symbols by testing them operationally at the level of word and rhetoric. They must be revelational not expository. When the words begin to come easily the symbol takes shape through them, and the basic rhetoric of the poem asserts itself; *e.g.*, mode, genre, line-length, rhythm, tone, *etc.* At some point during this initial stage of writing, the symbols feel "right" and the poem proceeds, with the poet working at both levels simultaneously, making the minor symbol-clusters come together, glow through the words asserting them. Riel, for example, begins to work against the backdrop of prairie, Metis pantheism, Catholic mysticism and the set of counter-symbols represented by Sir John A., the Orange order, Ottawa politics, *etc.*, and the whole design begins to emerge. At this point, the underlying myths may begin to be felt–like shadows, tensions, mirrors within mirrors. Seen from afar, their outline is simple, as Frye suggests: a quest, a tyrannical father over-thrown, the rape of innocence, a prideful fall. To see myth in these general, critical terms is a useful activity, providing the reader with a framework for his reading which is as wide and as deep as the human psyche itself, and a backdrop for those myths which he will encounter "live" within the work of art.

For what I have been trying inadequately to describe above is the poet's discovery of the *myth alive* and the reader's rediscovery of these identifying symbols as he reads. In its living state, the myth is not simple in substance or in outline (though an outline is visible and can be generalized); it is web, and filigree, and labyrinth–where the spaces mean as much as the lines. It is the structure on which all the rest has been built, and yet can only be felt through the flesh it gives shape to. But to call it structure is not wholly accurate, for it has force, and power, a potentiality for movement, for generation. So that the poet, even as he feels his poem close around the myth and reveal it, is aware that the structure is but a temporary arresting, the live myth caught and held, for the moment.

Let me illustrate again from my poem "Riel: a Poem for Voices." As I read the story of Riel in several source books, I knew I had to write a poem about him. Even as I read, I could see images coming up at me, could hear words and phrases rehearsing themselves in my head, could even sense the broad outlines of symbolic patterns, a glimpse of the myths lurking below. So, the poem began, not at the beginning, but in the middle and moving toward either end. As the words came and the form coalesced (dramatic/narrative, individual voices, long line modulating to short line and first-person lyrics, *etc.*), and major symbols developed, the poem took its own final shape–which turned out to be quite different from what I had initially envisaged. What I asked myself, on more than one occasion as the poem neared completion, was "How do I know when it is finished?" (I had long ago written Riel's "last" speech), "What force or pattern is governing the selection of materials at this late stage?" Near the beginning of work, after the initial groping, you feel that you are making some conscious decisions, but as it progresses, you seem to work more blindly and yet less arbitrarily, feeling your way, though the way is not necessarily more difficult. Well, "Riel" ended when the last piece was fitted, and I sensed for the first time that the whole thing was about (characters, incidents, images, words, rhetoric, *etc.*). I felt those myths which had given my poem shape; that were, in the deepest sense, its meaning. And even now, I have to go back and re-read the poem myself if I wish to feel its original power. You can't seem to carry live myths very far. We have suitcases full of dead ones.

What has the foregoing got to do with Canadian mythology and nationalism? Just this. The myths in genuine literature are honest. They are deep identifying symbols. Our literature, and the mythology it embodies, is thus a repository of "national" symbols. It will help to explain what we are. It will not *create* an identity for us, but will reveal the one we already have.

To be more specific about how this works: each symbol in a poem is at first a *private* one, subsumed by the personality and words of the poet. But it is also public, just as language itself is both personal and social, relevant and absolute. The words are the poet's, but they belong to others as well, and they *mean* in ways beyond his control. By the mere act of identifying himself through the medium of language, the poet has made his work and that part of himself involved in it, public property. In this light, the discussion between public and private symbols is irrelevant; they are merely more or less recognizable. The point here is that the works of our poets are public documents to be read so thoroughly that the myths shine through. Secondly, the poet, as person, is one of us, part of this nation, having shared the same environment, the same values, the same history, the same schooling; thus, his person, or self-speaking the language of the self, will be *other* than us, but an other more like us than we might suspect or hope. His words, his symbols, his myths will be identifiable and identifying in the only way that humans have of sharing experience and defining themselves as a social group. Our literature is there, and it is important.

The myths which it embodies are significant in at least two ways. First, a wide reading in our literature, set against a background of the best in English literature, will reveal the kinds of myth common to our time and place (past and present); that is to say, that out of the whole range of possible human myths, Canadian writers have chosen these kinds. For example, can we not learn a considerable amount about ourselves by discovering that pastoral myths have always been of prime interest to our poets and novelists? Or that, as Frye and others have noted, there is a distinctly apocalyptic tendency in our best literature. Journeys and quest abound. On the other hand, we don't find many Ulros or neon jungles (not yet). In brief, this kind of criticism, in which myth is generalized for the sake of analysis and comparison, is a valuable way for a nation to begin to discover its "lost" identity.

But the second way is much more significant and valuable, and is the one I am particularly promoting. It involves coming at the *myth alive* and experiencing it both emotively and intellectually. Any analysis of such myths would entail comparing the subtle and elusive differences between this pastoral myth and that one–the pastoral quality or feeling of *Sunshine Sketches* and, say, the peculiar nature of many of our quest which are essentially different from their American counterparts; where the enemy is more likely to be space, the nothingness of north, where the dominant feeling may be a sense of estrangement from the mother-culture, and the illumination at the end no more than an existentialist glow. It is at this level of reading and criticism that literature will yield to us its identifying icons, where the *myth alive* is felt through the individual work, and compared, both instantaneously and in retrospect, with other works of similar scope and power. For here one comes closest to touching the meaning sought after by both poet and reader. Here one catches the unique identity of the individual poet in the very act which makes that identity a public and universal artefact. I may have "chosen" Louis Riel as a private symbol and worked him into a poem in order to discover certain things about myself, but the language I was compelled to work in, indeed the symbols themselves (Riel, Sir John A., the events of 1870-85) belonged from the outset to the people of Canada. So, the poem is at once intensely private and hopelessly public. As a Canadian of a certain type, what I discovered about myself is also what is there for each Canadian to discover, or rediscover, for himself.

Before this starts to sound overly pompous, let me just say that what one finds in the literature may be trivial or important. It depends on the work. But all serious literature will yield information of *some* significance. Let us once and for all set aside the irrelevant arguments about "quality"; let us temper our paranoic inclinations, and seek to eradicate the neo-colonialist sensibility within each of us; in brief, let us get on with the job of taking our literature seriously, of reading it deeply and widely, of developing a genuine critical tradition in which mythology is given its just due. And since criticism, as Frye has noted, is ninety per cent concerned with teaching, let us promote our literature and its mythology throughout the school system. Let us teach it until it speaks for itself.

The country we discover will be our own.

– 10 –

Literature and Reading:
The Cognitive Dimensions

Indirections (O.C.T.E.) VII, 2 (Spring 1982)

I

The psycholinguistic research of the past years has provided us with a set of hypotheses about how children acquire language, develop competency in it, and use it as a principal means through which early reading and writing are achieved. (Smith 1978, de Villiers 1979, Cramer 1978). The belief that reading is merely (or even initially) decoding words has been seriously challenged and the parts-to-whole methodology associated with it largely debunked (Holdaway 1979, chs. 1-3). The effects of these shifts in perspective have yet to work their way through the primary and junior classrooms of the country, and while that process is occurring, it seems an appropriate moment to look farther up the educational continuum to see what effects the psycholinguistic hypotheses about reading might have on the curriculum for grades seven to twelve.

It is at grade seven, of course, that many language arts teachers begin to think of themselves as English teachers and the word "literature" appears in government guidelines and in courses of study. Before that, it seems, students "read" from a reader, and reading itself is only one corner of the language quadrivium. More important, from a purely cognitive perspective, it is in grade seven (when students are about twelve years of age) that the first of a series of profound changes takes place. Whichever of the major schools of cognitive development one defers to, age twelve is cited as significant: for Piaget it marks the onset of formal operations and the development of a sophisticated sense of time; for Vygotsky and Luria it denotes the beginning of a series of confrontations with more abstract, adult concepts (see Desjarlais and Rackauskas 1974, pp. 183-206 for a detailed discussion); for Bruner it signals a movement away from the iconic stage towards the abstract/linguistic one (1966, ch. 1); and for Moffett it rings the first note of genuine self-consciousness about thinking and allows the student to begin expressing himself with decreasing dependency on the ego and its associated forms, drama and narrative (1968, chs. 1-2). It is not surprising, then, to find the schools beginning to emphasize in grade seven the "objective" study of history, geography, and, of course, literature. Whether or not this course of action is justified in the light of other realities, it makes sense from the narrow cognitive view.

In the schools, however, the transition from what I would describe as a reflexive, responsive and egocentric mode of processing "experience" (in the case of reading the experience is a reader's encounter with a text) to a reflexive, analytic, and sociocentric one is often handled abruptly or simply not acknowledged. For many students, entering the English classroom of junior high (grade seven) or high school (grade nine or ten) is a jolting and confused affair. Many go from a reading class to a "lit" class with no special preparation for the shift and little appreciation by their teachers that reading and literature are often conceived of and taught in ways which are contradictory. In fact, our failure to define clearly for ourselves the appropriate relationship between reading and literature may prevent us from implementing a genuine developmental curriculum from K to 12– despite the opportunities presented by the psycholinguistic models now taking hold in some of the primary schools.

II

In what way is the traditional English/literature teacher also a teacher of reading? After all, high school teachers are notorious for insisting that they "teach poetry and Shakespeare and modern lit." And, of course, they do. When students are able to reflect on their own reading, monitor and edit their own first responses, and begin to see with increasing self-consciousness the role that form, genre, and theme play in the comprehension of texts–they too will feel more and more that they are studying a body of something or other with some kinds of recurrences and constraints (Gutteridge 1970). So, the story of English studies in high schools is often one of either gradual drift or quick cut from reading individual texts and mastering word-attack skills to the analysis of groups of poems, novels, or plays. The goals for courses in literature invariably include worthy statements about its moral dimensions, its psychological impact, its cultural relevance, its vicariously presented "universal" experience, and so on. Theme and genre groupings are common, with the implication that aspects of form and idea will emerge through comparative study. Lists of purely literary devices are not unusual: Petrarchan versus Shakespearean, dramatic irony, assonance, *et al.* For decades such goals have been the exclusive preserve and hallmark of the high school English teacher.

To a public worried by reported declines in the reading norms of high school graduates, however, the worthiness of literature-based courses is no longer self-evident. Perhaps all the emphasis on literature *per se*, with its apparent narrow linguistic focus and its vague and unmeasurable experiential goals, has skewed the language-learning enterprise in grades seven to twelve. The back-to-the-basics and language-across-the-curriculum movements are, in part, public response to this perceived distortion.

But what if the literature teacher, without her knowing it and provided she is doing her job well, is actually realizing a number of objectives not formally spelled out in the literature syllabus, ones which are fundamentally cognitive and have general significance across the curriculum? What if the successful teacher of *Hamlet* is really a reading teacher in a different guise? If so, then some genuine continuity between elementary and secondary school language learning could be achieved and the teaching of literature restored to its former lustre.

III

All reading is basically comprehension, and comprehending is essentially cognitive (Smith 1978, pp. 176-178; Gutteridge 1981). The validity of this hypothesis has now been demonstrated at the primary level (Holdaway 1979). There is no reason to assume that the process changes *in essence* as the reader matures. At the age of twelve or so a typical reader begins to become self-conscious about his reading. He feels more comfortable about comparing texts, seeing relationships and recurrences—that is to say, his general cognitive processing is evolving towards the categorical and the abstract. But the challenge to him as a reader does not change its primary focus: he has before him a text composed of words, sentences, and units of organization (paragraph, stanza, scrip-format, *etc.*). His initial task is unvarying: to make sense of that text as a collocation of words and their meanings. Hence, any literature teacher who wishes to have her students respond to the esthetic, moral, psychological, and cultural dimensions of a great novel can do so only if the students have been able to comprehend it first. These *experiential* (non-cognitive) goals for English, laudable as they may be, *are either outcomes of comprehension or co-extensive with it.* They may be realized during the reader's initial response, the subsequent analysis, or consequent discussion; but they cannot be said to be genuinely achieved if large parts of the text are still incomprehensible to many of the students. This claim may seem tautological, but when one sees lists of literary devices on a syllabus or an examination, one must conclude that these are seen as "add-on" objectives. That is, the literature teacher takes the grade-nine student who has already somehow learned the "basics of reading" and supplements with more "advance" *literary* devices and their associated tasks. Some version of this unstated assumption seems to underlie and distort much literature teaching in high school. Moreover, it leaves the teacher there vulnerable to the charge that "reading tactics" are being depreciated at the expense of device-hunting and theme-pursuit. Hence, it is imperative that *comprehension be reinstated as the continuing, primary, and necessary act of all reading experiences, literary or otherwise.* The goals that flow out of and support comprehension, though worthy in themselves, are second-order considerations.

IV

All successful literature teachers, then, are *ispso facto* teachers of reading. But how does the seemingly narrow focus on the fictional modes in English classes lead to an orderly and continuous development of a student's general competence in comprehension? We may assume that the elementary-school student has become familiar with the strategies needed to comprehend straightforward stories and to a lesser extent uncomplicated passages of exposition; his experience with poems and play-scripts may have been intermittent and most likely participatory (acting out, choral performance). If in high school he merely continues to read more exposition, fiction, poetry and drama, what new or deeper or more refined comprehension skills is he learning? One answer, as we have seen, is that a sort of enrichment takes place with the *addition* of special devices heretofore unexplored plus more "knowledge about" genres and typical themes (ballads rhyme abab, epiphanies proliferate). A more appropriate answer, however, might be that the cognitive processing required for *any* kind of comprehension-of-text is merely developed further *as an extension of what has already been initiated.* The study of literature as an extending and deepening of comprehension *per se* may be illustrated by reference to at least four phenomena that should occur in a properly conceived English program. Two of these are strictly cognitive and two are closely allied general strategies.

GENERIC QUESTIONS

As soon as an adolescent reader shows signs of being able to tolerate and then voluntarily initiate a "second reading" of a text, he begins, as Frank Smith has noted (1978, p. 178) to raise in a conscious way new kinds of questions (aided by the teacher) whose answers deepen his understanding of a text. Questions about the language as language and about the formal shape of text (the rhetoric) begin to yield meanings the maturing reader could only guess at previously. For example, in a grade-nine literature class students might, within a single week, have studied a short story like Carl Stephenson's "Leiningen Versus the Ants" and a lyric poem like the one below:

ICE

When Winter scourged the meadow and the hill
And in the withered leafage worked his will
The water shrank, and shuddered, and stood still—
Then built himself a magic house of glass,
Irised with memories of flowers and grass,
Wherein to sit and watch the fury pass.
—Charles G. D. Roberts*

In reading the story, students would not think of decoding it word by word or sentence by sentence. Their implicit and unarticulated knowledge of story-form is vast and sure; they have been read stories as infants, teethed on them in grade one, and encountered them each year thereafter. Moreover, their response to thousands of television shows and films has provided constant reinforcement of the conventions of narrative "fiction," and much of the anecdotal talk inside school and out has involved students in story-telling. By grade nine, advanced readers will be more conscious of these conventions and the linguistic cues signaling them; less experienced readers will still be able to call upon prior knowledge (implicit) to begin predicting at least the story-line. Typical reader-questions at this stage for a story like "Leiningen" might include: "Why is this Leiningen so cocky even though the ants sound terrifying?", "These seem like unusual ants, but then we're in South America, aren't we?", "The ants are almost like computers or machines—is that going to be important?", "I've read this sort of thing before; maybe this one'll be about man defeating nature or about a braggart getting his come-uppance." Indeed, the experienced literature-teacher-cum-reading-teacher will arrange her lesson to elicit such questions from students or will raise them herself where appropriate. Questions prompted equally by the actual words on the page and by the reader's expectations based on previous reading and on knowledge of the world—these are the signs that indicate a student has reached the edge of the plateau that was beyond his grasp perhaps only two years before. Questions prompted this way by the text—a set of running interrogatives in the head—are, of course, a key aspect of cognitive processing: words and the forms they assume trigger questions which are then answered in a series of mental operations we can only infer through our monitoring of student talk and analysis of our own thinking-as-we-read.

Little wonder, then, that grade nines not only enjoy "Leiningen" but find it easy to comprehend with minimal prompting from teacher. But a few days later when the poem "Ice" is given out and students are asked to read it over once or twice and be prepared to tell what it is about, the response is almost certain to be different from that which would be given if the same question were asked of the story. Most grade nines, even advanced readers, are inexperienced with poetry. Even if they have, against the odds, read some poetry with enthusiasm in elementary school, the reinforcing factors that deepened the sense of the story-form and made so much of that reading "automatic" are absent. In "Ice" there is, at best, only a rudimentary story, signaled by "when" and "then." To the grade-nine reader some things do happen here, but the powerful cause-and-effect pattern of much fiction is missing. The impact of character and dialogue—so helpful in the comprehension of stories even when the words are difficult (as in "Leiningen")—is vague or strange. Winter is a character, and maybe water is too, and they conflict a bit, but what does it all mean? Such is the probable pattern of second-questioning in the student's head. Lacking the predictive ease of "Leiningen," "Ice" would drive some students to word-by-word decoding where "leafage" and "Irised with memories" might be more daunting than they need be; others will apply what story features they can and at least "see" what happens; a few will develop "tunnel vision" (Smith 1978, p. 29) and give up. Why should this be so? Why should a poem whose vocabulary is much less difficult than that of a story be harder to comprehend than the latter? The answer, in part, is that comprehension is neither a set of global competencies nor a static learning phenomenon. Knowing how to read stories—using predictive measures derived from past encounters—will not guarantee that a student will be able to read a poem (or a play or novel or editorial). A wide vocabulary drawn from reading fiction would allow a student to decode the words and sentences in "Ice," see the embedded story, respond eclectically to some of the connotative diction—but little more. What more is there? Is this merely a rich description of the formation of ice, poeticized through Personification (the Big Device in grades seven and eight)?

There is much more as any mature reader of poetry knows. What the naive readers in grade nine could not yet ask themselves were questions about patterning; *e.g.*, the two sets of rhyming tercets indicate two "stanzas" or "scenes." The mood of the first scene is opposite that of the second (which represents an action following on the first one). The pattern of harsh sounds and progressive imagery of scourge and shrinkage and death are set against the generative image-pattern ("built," "Irised") and softer sounds. An appropriate reading of these two events, freighted with connotative meanings and related by an ironic cause-and-effect, must be allegorical as well as narrative. The water draws on its memories of beauty past to create a new kind of garden in which to wait out the winter. Having got this far, the veteran reader of verse begins to explore some of the extended meanings he has learned to expect from that mode: the possible ironies of the title; the notion of Nature's cycle and ultimate futility of Winter's scourge; perhaps the scourging is a necessary part of a death-rebirth sequence. And so on.

The point here is that any reader who is willing to approach poetry will have to learn to make major adjustments in how he goes about getting meaning: knowing the words is requisite but not adequate; transposing general tactics extrapolated from encounters with other modes will be of important but limited value. Lyric poetry requires a reader to expect such things as a meaningful use of sound, rhythm and phrase-shaping; a pattern of arrangement which cannot be instantly predicted (embedded story or drama, contrast, monologue of thought/feeing, *et al.*); the continual movement towards connotation, allegory, metaphor, and extended meanings; and, of course, more ambiguity than most fiction. Learning how to use the cues given in the text to formulate the special questions inherent in these features requires a broadening and deepening of the cognitive processing used in comprehension. Being able merely to recognize similes or rhyme schemes is in no way equivalent to raising the complex interweaving of questions illustrated above. If the literature teacher is able to help students raise such legitimate questions, she is not merely grafting "literary" concepts onto some hypothetical, general reading base: rather, she is calling on her students to extend *anything* they already know about reading and experience into the less familiar landscape of the poem—to discover what is unique to that genre and what can be safely transferred from related ones. The learning involved in this exercise is no little achievement; and while it remains essentially cognitive, it may well be the ensuing pleasures and uses of reading that will most impress the student.

VARIANT QUESTIONS WITHIN A GENRE

Cognitive growth is also achieved when students continue to read widely within a single genre. The proponents of mastery learning would have us believe that certain concepts derived from reading are learned completely by certain ages (or ought to be). Indeed, some literature teachers themselves "stage" the introduction of literary terms with such a premise in mind: simile in grade seven, metaphor in grade eight, omniscient narrator in grade eleven, and symbolism in grade twelve. Insofar as the concepts these terms represent are related to other validated stages in cognitive growth (*e.g.* personification is likely an easier form of metaphor for young readers to grasp because it is closer to the iconic or concrete stage of mental operations). But such exceptions distort the most important issue: is a concept like plot or story-line ever fully learned? Is it mastered when a grade-six student can define it on a test or summarize the plot of a given story? That general concepts–about time, cause and effect, selectivity/highlighting–are learned from reading fiction (and other modes) is not in doubt. But are such general concepts static? Or do they evolve in some way? The most probably hypothesis is that broad concepts like plot, metaphor, irony, viewpoint, and temporality–all prompted in whole or in part by reading literature–begin very early as gross concepts and are refined by successive encounters with texts (the notion of over-extension: see Moffett 1968, ch. 2 and deVilliers 1979, pp. 31-39) governed by appropriate teaching and subject to the general constraints of cognitive development.

For example, a grade one student may have already acquired an unconscious but powerful sense of "plot;" *i.e.*, he responds to strongly plotted stories; if they get too expository or didactic, he may fall asleep. (Watch young students viewing films and you will see a familiar pattern of response: intense interest in narrative and boredom with commentary or talkiness.) This student knows what plot is though he cannot discuss it as a concept (by grade two or three he'll give a re-tell). The concept at this stage is gross: it encompasses only emphatically plotted texts; stories with a more subtle line of cause and effect or a rearranged chronology may be classed as "non-story." When more kinds of stories have been encountered and talked out (with the aid of a teacher), the "new" aspects of plot are drawn through the existing concept so that the latter must become not more general but more abstract. That is, the refined concept will have more discriminating power because it accommodates more sub-types, and as the sub-types themselves bifurcate under the pressure of fresh encounters, the category itself becomes more rarefied, more reliable in its application, and more open to subsequent adjustment.

In the reading of imaginative literature *per se*, three variables would appear to govern concept formation and development: the nature of novel texts (they must challenge the current belief); the readiness principle that seems to constrain certain aspects of cognitive development (sense of historical time, concrete to formal operations, ability to interpret metaphor structurally); and the nature of the encounter with a novel text (including the mediation of the teacher as mature reader and sensitive pedagogue, other context factors: stress, self-image). As long as these variables are attended to, then the exploration of a single genre (like the short story) across the entire continuum from grades one to twelve will continue to promote cognitive growth. In brief, a reader does not "learn" the short story and then move on to other challenges. Nonetheless, since each genre has some rhetorical features unique to it, both generic variety and sustained focus on a single type will yield ongoing, positive results.

V

Besides helping to develop specific cognitive processing skills across a range of genres and promoting continuous and general concept attainment, the literature teacher sets up and maintains an appropriate environment in which such learning can occur.

BEHAVIOURAL ADJUSTMENTS

Students not only have to adjust comprehension strategies in moving from genre to genre, they must also make behavioural accommodations. In reading fiction, for example, students need to adjust their mind-set or predisposition when facing short as opposed to long fiction. The literary short story often requires several careful and complete readings, at a slow and deliberate pace, with a tolerance for initial confusion; conversely, the classic novel may demand selective re-reading of parts, a confidence to read ahead when puzzled (turning back is a last resort since most novels are cumulative and richly redundant), and a special patience with a slowly evolving plot. In moving from fiction to poetry a reader's behavioural adjustment may be more dramatic for poetry calls for a tolerance of ambiguity, paradox and ambivalence; an acceptance of the non-synonymous nature of much verse (quite often one must know all the words with all their meanings); and a much-reduced context. As Smith has pointed out in reference to beginning readers (p. 97), such psychological factors intrinsic to the nature of the reading act, are often as important determinants of successful comprehension as so-called decoding tactics. Even with the vastly more experienced high-school reader, these kinds of adjustments–essentially behavioural or dispositional–are important. The teacher will need to provide a mature model for her students to emulate, as well as attempt to create a reading environment that will prompt the appropriately adjusted behaviour.

READING FALLACIES

Finally, the high school student, faced by a variety of literary/fictional forms and an increasing number of discursive/non-fictional ones in the subject areas, can be dazzled by yet another set of imperatives to which he must adjust as a reader. I refer to what are loosely known as reading or literary fallacies. These are both general and unique to individual genres. For example, poetry induces among some students the Literal Fallacy ("I only see a telephone pole, not Christ's cross!") or its opposite, the Allegorical Fallacy ("There's no pole there at all, only Christ's cross"). (See Gutteridge 1972 for a full discussion of these and others). Highly poetic fiction, when first encountered, often raises the literal fallacy once again. Many students want all stories to be "real," yet believe that poetry is all "fantasy." The student who worries obsessively about the genesis of Lady Macbeth's children will have trouble truly enjoying Shakespeare's *Macbeth*. Similarly, when sophisticated argument or exposition is first encountered, some students believe that because it is non-fiction it is somehow more "real" and certainly more "true." What each of the various fallacies indicates is the existence of a genuine problem associated with comprehending genres whose features are often unique, not only linguistically but epistemologically. Poems demand from us a special set of validation procedures and make a special appeal to our sense of belief in what is and what is not (Frye 1963, ch. 3)–quite different from how we accept an editorial or go about validating our interpretation of it. Surreal fiction imposes on our credulity in ways much more demanding than the documentary novel. What is true, what is real, what is valid are questions that inform all properly conceived literature programs. Learning how to apply the "rules" associated with these questions to a full range of genres–fiction and non-fiction–begins with an appropriate sense of how to get meaning-from-text. The so-called fallacies are merely symptoms of more basic problems with comprehension or the pedagogy used in aid of it (sometimes, that is, *teachers* induce the fallacies; see Gutteridge 1976). Fallacies may also signal difficulties with the psychological stance required to allow the mind to begin operating on a text. In either case, the literature teacher who makes every effort to mitigate the effects of these fallacies is acting also as a reading teacher: she is bringing to bear on the issue all she knows about the nature of the reading process itself. No mere appeal to lofty literary ideals will do: the dispensing of poetic licenses or exhortations to "suspend your disbelief or else" cannot replace a detailed and discriminating knowledge of which aspects of the reading process to address at which time.

VI

Although the foregoing analysis is merely an outline of the relationship that appears to exist between literature and reading, some implications for teaching and further research may now be clear:

1. Although due attention must still be given to subject matter, theme, and teacher preference in the selection of literary works, the cognitive demands of the text are of paramount importance. If students must be challenged by increasingly novel texts for cognitive gains to be made, the nature of those challenges and their appropriateness to specific grades and classes must be better defined. Current readability measures are obviously inadequate, as are obsolete notions of "literary devices" or the so-called "mastery" of reading concepts.

2. Although all normal students seem to move from concrete to abstract/formal operations around grade seven, they do not do so simultaneously nor in a uniform manner. What determines a cognitive challenge for a grade-nine student who has read a hundred books a year since grade five will be decidedly different from that for the one who has annually skimmed six required tests. Though all reading comprehension is essentially cognitive, its development depends exclusively on successive *encounters*, no encounters, no progress. Hence, not all grade-nine courses need be the same; if students are of mixed ability, then some differentiated reading tasks and other assignments may be necessary.

3. By the same token, cognitive does *not* imply the obsessive use of analytic pedagogy, an academic   approach (in the worst sense), learning abstractions without a rich data-base, nor a weakening of the experiential/moral dimensions of reading literature. Grade twos chanting Blake's "Tyger! Tyger!" and then illustrating the poem (see the B.B.C. film of the same name) are enmeshed in cognitive processing as surely as grade twelves analyzing Hamlet's "To be or not to be."

4. All methodologies in current use must be re-examined to see whether they promote the appropriate comprehension strategies, dispositions and behaviours.

5. Some literature teachers may have to learn more about cognitive development and especially early reading in order to reorient their teaching along the lines suggested above.

6. The value of standardized tests and other forms of objective testing which rely exclusively on the assumption that reading skills are global (with easy transfer across modes and genres) will have to be scrutinized. The implications of the arguments in this paper make it clear that a student could score very highly on an objective test with discursive passages and still be   functionally illiterate when faced with a poem. Such anomalies need to be addressed more vigorously than they have been in the past.

7. The notion, somewhat fashionable nowadays, that literature teachers should be replaced by specialists trained exclusively in remedial or developmental reading may once and for all be dismissed. If reading skills are being poorly taught in a school or system, it is precisely because the literature teachers are not teaching *literature* appropriately. As we have seen, a properly conceived approach to reading poems and stories (and novels, plays, fables, articles, and editorials) will of necessity and by definition help students develop general concepts and cognitive processes specific to reading. Furthermore, larger questions of an epistemological and ontological nature may also be involved. And all this with no diminution of the traditional and cherished objectives for literature. Conversely, no "reading teacher," untutored in the issues associated with the response to imaginative works of all kinds, could replace the genuine teacher of literature.

8. In the *senior* high school where the notion of genre broadens yet again to include categories governed by the needs of the academic disciplines that rely heavily on reading and writing–history, geography, man-in-society, religion, economics, some parts of the sciences–the literature teacher will share the burden with her colleagues. In this sense language across the curriculum is an idea whose time has come. Nonetheless, several points should be kept clearly in mind. Only a minority of high-school students is enrolled in truly academic courses with advance reading demands; for the majority of students, engaged in general or vocationally directed programs, reading development is still at the level of the rhetorical and generic, the behavioural and dispositional. Moreover, up to the age of fifteen or so, almost all students prefer to read–in class and out–the various fictional forms (Purves and Beach 1972, pp. 71-81; Burdenuk 1978); many non-academic students, when encouraged, simply extend this predilection by several years or a lifetime. Hence, *novels and stories represent the only major quantitative base our students have* from which to derive linguistic concepts and on which to try out their developing cognitive skills. In terms of resident expertise the English teacher holds unchallenged sway over two of the four modes of written expression – Narrative (prose fiction, story-poems, fables) and Description (lyric poetry, aspects of prose fiction)–and shares the other two–Drama (with a close cousin or under her other hat) and Exposition (criticism, exclusively, and other forms of discursive pose with colleagues in history, geography, *etc.*) Language across the curriculum–as far as reading goes–means a shared enterprise among a number of teachers with special expertise: but because of the pattern of students' reading preferences and the nature of reading development itself, the literature teacher perforce will carry much of the responsibility for many of the students most of the time.

These issues and the accommodations suggested to meet them must be considered soon if we are to avoid the only possible alternative: programmed learning in cramped cubicles without sunlight or fresh air or the spontaneous speech of the individual imagination.

REFERENCES

– Bruner, Jerome. S. *Toward a Theory of Instruction.* New York: Norton, 1966.

– Burdenuk, Jean. "Adolescents and Recreational Reading." *In Review: Canadian Books for Children.* Summer 1978. pp. 5-18.

– Burstall, Christopher, dir. *Tyger, Tyger, an Enquiry into the Power of a Familiar Poem.* B.B.C. Films, 1969.

– Cramer, Ronald I. *Children's Writing and Language Growth.* Columbus, Ohio: Merrill, 1978.

– Desjarlais, I. and Rackasukas, J.A., *Needs and Characteristics of the Students in the Intermediate Years, Ages 12-16.* Ottawa: University of Ottawa Press, 1974.

– Frye, Northrop. *The Well-Tempered Critic.* Bloomington: Indiana University Press, 1963.

– Gutteridge, Don. "Teaching Structure in English." *The English Quarterly,* III, 2. (June 1970). pp. 35-48.

– Gutteridge, Don. "The Affective Fallacy and the Student's Response to Poetry." *English Journal,* LXI, 2. (February 1972), pp. 210-221.

– Gutteridge, Don. "The Hidden Meaning Syndrome." *The English Quarterly,* IX, 1 and 2 (Spring Summer 1976), pp. 29-35.

– Gutteridge, Don. "Teaching Literature For Cognitive Development: A Double Perspective." *Indirections,* VI, 3 (Fall 1981), pp. 28-40.

– Holdaway, Don. *The Foundations of Literacy.* Sydney: Ashton Scholastic, 1979.

– Moffett, James. *Teaching the Universe of Discourse.* Boston: Houghton-Mittlin, 1968.

– Purves, Alan C. and Beach, Richard. *Literature and the Reader.* Urbana, Ill.: N.C.T.E., 1972.

– Smith, Frank. *Understanding Reading,* 2nd edition. New York: Holt Rinehart, 1978.

– deVilliers, Peter A. and Jill G. *Early Language.* Cambridge: Harvard University Press, 1979.

Afterword by Brian T. W. Way

On First Looking into
The View from Darien

Then felt I like some watcher of the skies
When a new planet swims into his ken;
Or like stout Cortez when with eagle eyes
He star'd at the Pacific—and all his men
Look'd at each other with a wild surmise—
Silent, upon a peak in Darien.
　　　—excerpt "On First Looking into Chapman's Homer"
　　　John Keats 1816

John Keats and Charles Clarke, his friend and former teacher, sat up late one October evening in 1816 reading a copy of George Chapman's translation of Homer (published about two centuries earlier but previously unread by the poet); by breakfast, Keats placed a new sonnet before Clarke, simply entitled "On First Looking into Chapman's Homer." Homer's works were certainly known to Keats and his generation mostly through the efforts of eighteenth-century writers such as Dryden and Pope in brilliant though heavily formulaic, scholarly and stylized translations, but Chapman's Renaissance-era work to Keats was "loud and bold"—much freer, muscular, earthy and direct—to Keats, it was "pure serene" (proleptic, perhaps, of Shelley's "intense inane"). The poet likens this fresh discovery of Homer to that of the explorer Hernán Cortez's first sighting of the vast Pacific (actually, the explorer was Balboa—perhaps an error, but just as likely Keats felt a two-syllable name made for a crisper fit). Whoever the man, 'Cortez' and his company, like Keats, are rendered awestruck by their discovery, all left "Silent, upon a peak in Darien." For Keats, such silence represents the sustaining and magical essence of the written art, as he so eloquently proclaims elsewhere: "Heard melodies are sweet, but those unheard / Are sweeter still; therefore, ye soft pipes, play on; / Not to the sensual ear, but, more endear'd, / Pipe to the spirit ditties of no tone…" In silence, then, the poem, itself, stands as an homage to creativity and to education, a kind of literary palimpsest, one layer affixed to another like burning coals in a hearth—we read Keats' poem, Keats reads

George Chapman, Chapman translates the poetry of Homer, Homer recounts songs and stories he has heard from wandering poets, they, themselves, recalling and reconstructing tales told and retold through courts and villages about an ancient conflict among Greeks and Trojans and their gods. It is only through the literary act of words on the page or in memory, through "ditties of no tone," that one manages to travel the realms of gold. As such, literature is always a sustaining but mutable experience brought to being by a reader, to be visited and revisited over time—literature is renewed in our reading, and rereading, and we are renewed by it, a lifelong reciprocal process that is quite often inaugurated in, and sustains, a classroom setting. In the end, be it Homer, Chapman, or Clarke, "On First Looking into Chapman's Homer" is a poem by Keats for his teacher, and a poem about learning.

Don Gutteridge's *The View from Darien* is a self-selected collection of essays written and published during his time as Professor of Education at The University of Western Ontario; these essays date from thirty or more years ago, some as early as 1970, and all deal with ideas, problems and challenges particular to educational matters in that era. They are essays for teachers. Several interrogate specific curriculum documents and policies advocated by governments of the day, some present methods and lesson plans for teaching certain plays, poems and novels and still others tackle broader umbrella-issues such as the elusive idea of Canadian identity or pedagogical theories generally related to teaching reading and literature.

More specifically, in the first essay, "The Rudderless Ark," Gutteridge discusses pros, cons and changes needed in the guidelines established by the Ministry of Education in documents issued in the 1980s (especially the infamous 1987 *I/S Curriculum Guideline* that implausibly contained "two centres," Literature *and* Language). In "Teaching Literature for Cognitive Development," the focus is on streaming and the comparative difficulties of the literary works used. In "Shakespeare by Ear," a practical aural method for teaching Shakespeare's *Macbeth* is outlined; the next essay tackles the principles of questioning and question design—as teachers know (and lawyers, and police officers, and medical doctors, and *you name the discipline?*) there is no more important skill. "Setting Goals for English" returns to the issue of aims and objectives proposing an 'evaluation/accountability' model including an exemplar, a lesson outline for teaching Morley Callaghan's story, "Luke Baldwin's Vow" and in "The Drama of Literature in the High School Classroom," Gutteridge presents an epitomic model for teaching literature and achieving "significant behavioral change" with the teacher as mature reader, the student as apprentice and the text as a living entity. Next, a paper deals with the concept of affective fallacy and outlines reasons and methods to train students from falling into this sentiment—very much, a New Critical bent. "The Subject-Centred Curriculum" argues that education should be centred on subject matter rather than being student-centred, a compelling, albeit seemingly futile howl in the wilderness given the current post-Britton ethos of our classrooms. "Teaching the Canadian Mythology" takes up the debate over Canadian identity and offers an outline of the stages of composition in writing poems which, ultimately, may culminate in myth. Finally, "Literature and Reading in the High School," from 1982, works at defining the dichotomous relationship between being a teacher of reading and a teacher of literature.

Perhaps the question to be considered most with *The View from Darien* concerns the dimension of time—what, we may ask, is the relevance of topical essays that focus on specific issues and ideas, documents and scholarly arguments, contested some forty or fifty years ago? The curriculum documents, themselves, are long since discarded; and the issues of debate seem distant, an echo of things teachers used to think about. We know that education by its very essence is a mercurial thing, and especially so, it seems, in these last couple decades as students, teachers and schoolrooms, from AI to Podcasts to Zoom, have been swept up in a tsunami of technological, informational and social change. And, even beyond that, as teachers will assure you, while they may seek to convey in knowledge and skills the very best understandings of the past, the cultural pressure and the pedagogical impulse are always to shape and reshape lessons that embrace the present in the sacred hope of preparing students for that elusive and ever-extending future. In this regard, there is always a holy futility at the heart of teaching; it is a delicate balancing act, a kind of dream, partly truth and partly fiction (to quote the song), requiring the skill to treat all students equally but also individually, and always, in spite of the politics and the prospects, destined at best to teach the present and resist the illusive temptation to try to teach the future (which can never be done for none can know tomorrow). Temporal pressures, social expectations and an ever-expanding curriculum are always knocking on the classroom door. I think of the beguiling end of that most American of books we have so often taught in Canada, *The Great Gatsby,* which depicts a nation ever striving toward the future but, by that very act, inevitably falling farther from its dream:

> … Gatsby believed in the green light, the orgastic future that year by year recedes before us. It eluded us then, but that's no matter—tomorrow we will run faster, stretch out our arms farther. . . And one fine morning—
> So we beat on, boats against the current, borne back ceaselessly into the past.

So, again, what merit can be found in these time-bound discourses re-issued here as *The View from Darien.* Well, for one thing, we should always recall that standard chestnut, the oft-quoted (and often mis-quoted) wisdom of George Santayana: "Those who cannot remember the past are condemned to repeat it" (*The Life of Reason* 1905). Don Gutteridge's essays remind us (and show us) that, once in this province, teachers were actively engaged in considering and deciding what the goals of education should be and in designing how curriculum documents should be shaped, and they (and their students) benefitted from that cerebral process. There was an ownership at hand and a potentially deeper understanding of what lessons were fundamentally needed *and why.* Once upon a time draft documents were distributed to schools and collegial feedback requested—Premier Mike Harris's "common-sense" agenda radically changed that process. Between 1995 and 2002, the collection and redistribution of educational taxes were centralized (thus, neutering the role of the local Trustee and placing critical restrictions on Board governance), the actual number of Boards was drastically reduced (from 129 to 66 under the *Fewer School Boards Act, 1997*), the Department Head system was de-structured (generally, this system involved a group of experienced teachers which came to be perceived as a pedantic road bump slowing the advance of whatever new curricula and regulations were decreed) and standardized curricula, assessments and report cards were created and enforced province-wide without much local input. The unnecessary bureaucracy of the Ontario College of Teachers was also created, all part of a ubiquitous attempt at controlling and de-professionalizing teachers, a process that had been escalating, at least, since the 1980s in Ontario (remember that curious era, the time of Mulroney and Reagan and Thatcher, O My!). One of the great enemies to oligarchic control, of course, always resides in memory, in the recollection and rational debate of what has gone before, of what is and why, and of what may be gained, or lost, or wrought (for, as you know, "Oceania was at war with Eastasia. Oceania had always been at war with Eastasia."). A personal example comes to mind—around the turn of the millennium, as one of several Consultants for the London Board on loan as a writing team to the Ministry of Education, among many prohibitions, we were forbidden to include words/phrases like "culture" or "critical thinking" or to refer to any source in our research more than ten years old—at that time, nothing prior to 1990 was allowed (oops, I thought, there goes Socrates and Aristotle, and Arnold and Dewey and Montessori and Rosenblatt and Frye, too!). Fortunately, I suppose, the work of those teams was quickly buried in the work of other teams, and others, as one year turned into the next.

The View from Darien is packed with information that remains enlightening to anyone with an interest in the practice and theory of education. Case in point, several essays make reference to Bert Case Diltz. Diltz, a veteran of World War One, graduated from Queen's University with his Honours B.A., took an M.A. from Columbia and then went on to teach for decades at the University of Toronto where, from 1958 to 1963, he became Dean of the Ontario College of Education. In that post-war era, all who wanted to teach in Ontario were required to attend and acquire their qualification in a six-week summer course at O.C.E.; in the subject of English, they were trained by Diltz using a teaching method he had designed. By the late 1960s, Faculties of Education were formed and a full-year Bachelor of Education degree was required for teachers. Typically, the instructors hired at these new institutions were disciples of Diltz so the Diltzian method spread as gospel and, in certain ways, continues its influence to this day. As part of that process, Diltz published several theoretical books outlining his theories of teaching—*Pierian Spring* (1946), *The Sense of Wonder* (1953), *Patterns of Surmise* (1962), *Sense or Nonsense* (1972)—and edited numerous anthologies of poems and short stories, grammar and language texts, to provide school classrooms with the materials on which to practise his approach: *New Horizons* (1955), *Poetic Experience* (1955), *Word Magic* (1957), *Many Minds* (1963), *Frontiers of Wonder* (1968), among others. The Diltzian method was essentially a variation of the epistemological approach first introduced by Plato in his *Theaetetus* dialogue, commonly referred to as the Socratic method. In its purest form, Socrates asks questions of the student until the student comes to a clearer understanding of the issue him- or herself—the "answer," as such, ideally comes from the student, not from Socrates. Diltz's version has the teacher as the expert in the classroom asking question after question until the pupil arrives at the "correct" answer (in this case, generally, the teacher's answer). Diltz's books include numerous exemplars such as the following regarding Wordsworth's sonnet, "It is not to be Thought of"—("T" for Teacher; "P" for Pupil):

T: How far in the poem does the comparison extend?

P: To the word ever, and the first period, in the ninth line.

T: What purposes does the comparison serve?

P: It supplies the framework for the continuous flow of thought and emotiondown to the final period.

T: Whence comes this river?

P: From "dark antiquity."

T: Where is that on the map?

P: It is not a place but a time in history.

T: What is the significance of "dark"?

P: It suggests that freedom's source is prehistoric.

P: No record of its origin exists.

P: The spirit of freedom is very old.

T: Whither is the river flowing?

P: To "the open sea of the world's praise."

T: Where is that?

[and so on, from *Pierian Spring*]

Diltz was a product of his Modernist times. Modernism, with its adherence to science, a devotion to psychology, a love of literary irony and a preference for "dry, hard, classical verse," to use philosopher T. E. Hulme's phrase, dominated the literary sensibility of the first half of the twentieth-century (1890-1950). The ascetic prose and poetry of the likes of Joyce, Woolfe, Lawrence, Forester, Yeats, Eliot, Stevens and Pound set a gold standard, reinforced by the severe analytical platform of New Criticism driven by austere Formalist academics such as Ransom, Empson, Richards, Tate, Wimsatt, Brooks (and T. S. Eliot, too). This bent of criticism offered a clinical, no-nonsense (totalitarian) view of literary merit and translated into education by filling the English classroom with a lot of literary labels, from allegory to zeugma, advancing a scientific interpretation of how effective literature worked (Freytag's Pyramid or plot analysis triangles, or the like) and determining the need for an authority figure in charge of the class, that Diltzian expert (teacher with a capital "T"), a sage on the stage who knew the meaning of every literary work and, through precise questions, was able to guide his student-disciples accordingly. Interestingly, much of Diltz's final theoretical text, *Sense or Nonsense* (1972), reads like a cry of desperation, of defiance, a *rock of alarm* against a change that he sensed was coming:

> The psychologists and sociologists may classify and corral the less talented and encourage them to accept their lot, but they cannot make students of those who have little aptitude for learning. Must the whole system of education be modified in order to accommodate their whims or unstructured tantrums? Without restraining banks a river loses its identity. Whether the student works with language or with lathe, he is in school to organize and develop his mental faculties. The theorist, on the other hand, would drive him along the road to chaos without a creed.
>
> Whatever else is lost in the morass of experimenters, the study of literature must be preserved. It is time for those who believe in real education to stand fast together. The Scots have a lovely lilting word for it: *craigélachié*.

Although Diltz feared that "real education," as he labelled it, was disappearing, times do change, and no era seemed to change more visibly—Dylan went electric, hair got longer, skirts shorter, Canada found a flag, an identity and a literature, and television hit its stride—the electronic Age of Aquarius flowered, and the Global Village made all of us next-door neighbours. Postmodernism was afoot.

While English teaching probably owes a great deal to the dispassionate beat of Modernism (Eliot always claimed that the rhythm of a "tom-tom" sounded through all of his work—he liked the 'pun' with his name), another beat was also on the rise by the end of World War Two. Beat writers like Ginsberg, Kerouac and Burroughs, Confessionals such as Lowell, Plath and Purdy, Black Mountain devotees like Creeley, Dorn and Olson and counter-culture authors, Vonnegut, Brautigan, Barthelme, Gass, Coover, Kesey, Bukowski, Jong, Findley, Kroetsch, Marlatt, Wagamese, Barth, and a host of others, started to shake off the chains of Modernism in writing a fiction that challenged what was considered mainstream literature. Their Postmodern texts were personal, reflexive, flippant, metafictive and openly autobiographical; in step, critical stances began to accept the validity of personal response (phenomenologically, the implied reader) and myriad schools of criticism arose—Feminism, Marxism, Structuralism, Post-structuralism, Freudian, Jungian, Deconstruction, the Yale school, and so on. There is always a time-lag as cultures change, of course, so it was the 1970s and 1980s before Ginsberg's *Howl* appeared in *Norton Anthologies*, before Kerouac and Vonnegut and Kesey materialised on school courses, and before academics like Diltz sensed that change was blowing in the wind, that a "post-Diltzian era" had begun as Gutteridge phrases it in *Stubborn Pilgrimage* (1992), his comprehensive book about the Diltz Literary Method and the development of English teaching in Ontario. Accordingly, on several occasions in Gutteridge's *The View from Darian*, as it had been for Diltz, the climate of inevitable change seems ominously in the air; for example, one essay acknowledges:

> It is conceivable that in the long run we may lose the battle. But surely this is a less despairing thought than to contemplate the present situation, where, in the name of a factitious relevance or a fashionable but muddle-headed interdisciplinary approach, we see English lessons degenerate into debates on pollution or general discussions of sex and life (worthy as these might be in their own right). The decision to teach rests squarely on the shoulders of the individual teacher in his own classroom; and no amount of rationalizing about present cultural conditions will alter the fact.

Another begins:

> As an incurable believer in lost causes, I wish to argue in favour of a subject-centred school curriculum. Since my areas of competence are English and the school system of Ontario, they will form the basis for my argumentation, though I suspect that what I have to say will have broader implications. The timing of this paper may seem curiously anachronistic, yet it is precisely because of three recent developments in education that I feel we need a thorough reexamination [*sic*] of some of our basic premises and not a few of our assumptions and prejudices.

In another, considering the impact of the *Hall-Dennis Living and Learning Report* (1968), Gutteridge concedes: "Without question, English as a subject is adrift, and the implications of this drift must be studied with some care and purpose."

Initiatives in curricula such as that *Hall-Dennis Report* in Ontario were signs of the Postmodern and its impactful drift, in this instance a curriculum designed to give students a wide range of options, introducing new courses such as film study and Theatre Arts and encouraging the practice of team teaching, a rotary system of education for Grades Seven and Eight and open-concept schools. By the 1980s, while those initiatives sometimes sputtered and some educators resisted the change, others embraced what seemed inevitable and could be heard adopting phrases like "paradigm shift," essentially, another contextualized term for the Postmodern. In general, Postmodernism tended to question the certainty of twentieth-century (Modernist) scientific beliefs and offered fresh perspectives in everything from architecture and medicine to philosophy and literary criticism, and most certainly, education. Often, it tried to pull back the skin of culture to reveal and dissect the structures beneath. Conduits and support beams were now openly visible in newly constructed buildings, out-takes and bloopers were now part of film credits, *method acting* became mainstream, soup cans and comic strips depicted as art, deconstruction became the new new criticism, focusing as much on structure and semiotics and simulacra as on tropes and schemes and themes, photographs, drawings, advertisements, typographical variations, even questionnaires, were often now part of prose fiction and poetry (with authors sometimes showing up as characters in their own fiction as, one supposes, in some sense they always were), and education was suddenly imaged as a life-long activity that was somehow student-centred. In the Modernist classroom, students had unveiled the text to understand themselves and the world; now, in the Postmodernist classroom, students unveiled themselves to understand the text. (And classrooms continue to be filled these days with student-active projects and presentations supported by a variety of electronic programs like *Prezi* or *Google Slides* and all including aspects of pop culture, reflections on social media and reams of personal reflection.)

And so, as a whole *The View from Darian* places us in a remarkable time of transition from one era to the next and offers a portrait of a culture and its educational thought and method caught in an intriguing maelstrom of decision and indecision, of one ethos being swallowed by another. And what better way to understand the persistent growing pains of schooling that continue throughout our time than by direct immersion in the perceptions and insights, the words and ideas, of a contemporaneous scholar, thoughts always crafted by Gutteridge with spirit and integrity. Here we can experience first-hand theoretical and practical issues whose relevance is both timeless and transient, concerns that teachers of literature and reading and writing once considered and may well benefit from considering again. In education, while the present certainly trumps the past, the discourses and trends of the past are never irrelevant or far away—like Keats' poem, education is a palimpsest. In the classroom, we are always what we were, and more. Ideas by the likes of Socrates and Augustine, John Locke and Matthew Arnold, John Dewey and Louise Rosenblatt and Ivan Pavlov and John Comenius and Benjamin Bloom and Noam Chomsky and Maria Montessori and Nancie Atwell and Ken Goodman, and theoretical movements from Progressive Education to Feminism to Back-to-the-Basics to Excellence in Education to Whole Language to Choice Theory to the Social Justice Movement and Every Child Matters, all, and many more, stream like layered sunbeams through the ambience of our classrooms. As teachers, we do the best we can to inform ourselves comprehensively, and to inform our students as imaginatively and as sincerely as possible. One recalls the old folk adage:

> *you only come to know the true meaning of life*
> *when you plant a tree under whose shade*
> *you know you will never sit*

Such is teaching as *The View from Darien* reminds us, immersing us as it does in an illimitable discourse every bit as vast as the Pacific that Keats' explorers beheld so long ago with wild surmise and silence.

—Brian T. W. Way 2023

Brian T. W. Way was raised in Prince Edward County, Ontario, and attended university at Queen's, Waterloo, and Western. He spent his working life teaching at a variety of levels (elementary, secondary, college and university) and retired back to The County to creative endeavours, publications including *redirection, The Prince of Leroy, County Time, Bee, Somebody Should've told Fred, Hickory Tunes, magic birds, Perilous Journey in the Prose Fiction of Don Gutteridge.*

Don Gutteridge was born in Sarnia and raised in the nearby village of Point Edward. He taught High School English for seven years, later becoming a Professor in the Faculty of Education at Western University, where he is now Professor Emeritus. He has published seventy-six books: poetry, fiction and scholarly works in literary criticism and pedagogical theory and practice. He has published twenty-two novels, including the twelve-volume Marc Edwards mystery series and a YA fable, *The Perilous Journey of Gavin the Great*, and thirty-eight books of poetry, one of which, *Coppermine*, was short-listed for the 1973 Governor-General's Award. In 1970 he won the UWO President's Medal for the best periodical poem of that year, "Death at Quebec." Don lives quietly in London, Ontario.